T0139090

Security and Auditing of Smart Devices

Managing Proliferation of Confidential Data on Corporate and BYOD Devices

Internal Audit and IT Audit

Series Editor: Dan Swanson

Security and Auditing of Smart Devices

Managing Proliferation of Confidential Data on Corporate and BYOD Devices

Sajay Rai • Philip Chukwuma • Richard Cozart

CRC Press
Taylor & Francis Group
Boca Raton   London   New York

CRC Press is an imprint of the
Taylor & Francis Group, an **informa** business

CRC Press
Taylor & Francis Group
6000 Broken Sound Parkway NW, Suite 300
Boca Raton, FL 33487-2742

Printed on acid-free paper
Version Date: 20160923

International Standard Book Number-13: 978-1-4987-3883-5 (Hardback)

Library of Congress Cataloging-in-Publication Data

Names: Rai, Sajay, author. | Chukwuma, Philip, author. | Cozart, Richard, author. Title: Security and auditing of smart devices : managing proliferation of confidential data on corporate and BYOD devices / by Sajay Rai, CPA, CISSP, CISM, Philip Chukwuma, CISSP, Richard Cozart. Description: Boca Raton, FL : Taylor & Francis Group, LLC, CRC Press is an imprint of Taylor & Francis Group, an Informa Business, [2017] Identifiers: LCCN 2016027167| ISBN 9781498738835 (acid-free paper) | ISBN 9781498738842 (acid-free paper) Subjects: LCSH: Mobile communication systems--Security measures. | Mobile computing--Security measures. | Confidential business information--Protection. | Cell phone systems--Security measures. | Pocket computers--Security measures. Classification: LCC TK5105.59 .R35 2017 | DDC 621.3845/6028558--dc23 LC record available at https://lccn.loc.gov/2016027167

Visit the Taylor & Francis Web site at
http://www.taylorandfrancis.com

and the CRC Press Web site at
http://www.crcpress.com

Printed and bound in the United States of America by Sheridan

Contents

PART V   REPORTING, MONITORING, AND AUDITING

PART VI   SAMPLES

PART I

BENEFITS AND RISKS OF SMART DEVICES

This section will assist the readers to understand smart devices. Chapter 1 focuses on the definition of smart devices. Chapter 2 explains the differences between corporate-owned devices and bring your own devices. Chapter 3 discusses the types of data that reside on these smart devices. Chapter 4 identifies the benefits of using smart devices, and Chapter 5 discusses the risks of using smart devices.

So, let's get started.

1

DEFINITION OF A SMART DEVICE

1.1 Introduction

In developing countries, prior to the advent of cell phones and smart devices, the telephone was one of those things available only to the rich who could afford the official and unofficial price of owning one. It was a status symbol to own a landline phone. Then came cell phones and then smartphones. Communication became available to the masses, even in the developing countries. A street side vendor can now own a smart device and communicate with people far and wide. Just like the French Revolution liberated the French, smart devices have liberated the masses of the world. One wonders if IBM ever envisioned that *Simon*, the first cell phone, would be developed to become this global phenomenon.

What is this phenomenon that has so much global impact? So what is a smart device? How do we define a smart device? Ask many people, and you will get many devices that are included in the definition and many similar definitions. When defining a smart device, most people will immediately think of smartphones. Note, however, that we use smart devices here instead of just smartphones. While the definition of a smartphone as a smart device may be correct, it does not, however, identify and include various devices that may be defined as smart devices. The characteristics of a smart device are an important part of what a smart device is.

1.2 Characteristics of a Smart Device

A smart device must have certain characteristics to be identified as one. The characteristics of smart devices, at a minimum, include the following:

Connectivity: To be considered a smart device, the device must be connected to other devices, networks, appliances, and computer systems. This is possible because smart devices support various types of communication protocols, such as Wi-fi and Bluetooth. It must provide access to the Internet and have the ability to sync with multiple email accounts. The smart device must support virtual private networks (VPNs) for enterprises that require an additional layer of security to connect to the network. We hear the phrase *bring your own device (BYOD)*, and this phrase is being embraced by many companies. BYOD allows companies to provide access to their network infrastructure and data to employees' personal smart devices. In essence, the company is able to extend its network beyond company-owned devices. While this connectivity and the extension of the network increase productivity and reduce cost for the company, they come with the following threats and vulnerabilities:

- No physical control
- The use of untrusted devices and connection to untrusted networks
- The use of unknown content and applications created by unknown developers/publishers
- The use of location services

Interactive operation: This single attribute is the one reason why most people like smartphones and one of the main reasons that smartphones have been successful. If we say that desktops and laptops brought us the processing age, then we can safely say that smart devices brought us the access age. The interactive functions of a smart device include a touch screen for easy usability. It also includes a built-in keyboard that is either physical or software based. The built-in keyboard for smart devices has also led to an abbreviated form of texting communication language, which has substituted for the

Standard English language but is still an effective communication medium. Texting has become a new communication language with a growing vocabulary. Some examples of the texting language include acronyms such as oh my God (OMG) and adult in the room (AITR). The built-in keyboard has also led to the instant messaging mechanism. This instant messaging is used by most people instead of an email to quickly contact people and send messages.

Autonomous: A smart device must have the ability to process information and data on its own. This means that a smart device must have its own processor. This processor must run one of the most recognized operating systems such as Google's Android, Apple's iOS, Nokia's Symbian, or BlackBerry OS.

Form factor: The form factor for a smart device is very important. It must be small, thin, and considered sexy. The size will depend on whether the smart device is a phone, a tablet, or a watch. The form factor must be appealing, and, for this reason, smart device manufacturers spend a lot of time and money in improving the look of smart devices.

Multiple usages: For better usability, smart devices have built-in cameras for videos and still pictures. The picture functions have fueled a new culture of amateur publishers and instant publishing companies such as Twitter and Facebook. This ability with smart devices has also added words such as *selfie* to the English dictionary. With a smart device, a person can take a picture or record a video clip and instantly send that to friends or news media. It has made Twitter and Facebook the billion-dollar companies that they currently are because they have become the base of social media. Smart devices impact society in so many ways. The instant pictures and videos taken by people can also become evidence in court and an aid to the police. The cameras on smart devices raise questions about not only personal privacy but also a tool that can be used for potential corporate intellectual property theft.

Smart devices are also voice recorders, as well as a phone system. As such, they require a microphone for voice inputs. The microphones in smart devices have improved, and applications have been written to give voice commands to the smart device. Apple's Siri is a very good example. This further improves the ease of use of the smart device and provides some safety for people who have to use their smart device while driving. (Remember that it is highly recommended not to use your smart device while you are driving.)

In recent times, smart devices have also entered the financial arena and are used as an authentication mechanism. As a financial instrument, it allows payment for goods without cash or credit card through services like Square, GoPayment, and Apple Pay. These services are becoming accepted instruments and are supported by all the major banks.

In addition, smart devices have become an authentication mechanism to various information technology (IT) networks and systems. It is now a two-factor authentication mechanism. Because every employee has a smart device, companies can implement a two-factor authentication software on the mobile device and thereby improve access control to its IT infrastructure.

Electronic: The electronic characteristics of a smart device define the smart device as an object with an embedded memory for storage and processing power. As such, the smart device must have computing power. In fact, most of the smart devices currently out in the market have more computing power than most old computers. A 16-GB Samsung S5 or an iPhone 6, with 16 GB, has much more computing power than a TRS 80 or an IBM desktop that was made in the 1990s. As smart devices continue to evolve, the processors will continue to be faster, and the storage capacity will continue to increase. This continuous improvement is also blurring the line between laptops and tablets. For example, is Microsoft's Surface Pro 4 a laptop or a tablet? Or is it both because it performs both functions?

1.3 Definition of a Smart Device

So how do we define a smart device? Smart devices can be defined as an instant personal communication medium for the masses. It includes things such as smartphones, tablets, eReaders, smart watches, and smart eyeglasses. The list of smart devices will continue to grow as their adoption worldwide continues to grow, and new uses are developed. The application of smart devices also continues to grow and includes phones, photography, messaging, home, health monitoring, games, movie streaming, financial payment instrument, etc. as shown in the following list. What is apparent in this definition is that it does not include laptops.

Ever-growing list of smart device characteristics:
- Embedded memory
- Operating system (Android, iOS, etc.)
- Mobile browser
- Wi-fi
- Texting capability
- Digital cameras
- Remote control capabilities
- Synchronization with other devices
- Multitasking
- Internal storage
- Internet connection
- Hardware and/or software keyboard
- Touch screen
- Support for games
- Global Positioning System
- Email synchronization
- Third-party application support

eMarketer estimates the worldwide users of smartphones at 1.64 billion in 2014. But we know that smart devices include more than smartphones. Also, the graph in Figure 1.1 shows that, by 2018, the worldwide users of smartphones will grow to 2.56 billion.

The Pew Research Center estimates the following for American adults in 2014:

- About 58% have a smartphone.
- About 32% own eReaders.
- About 42% own tablets.

These numbers account for adults and do not include all the smart device ownership in the United States (Figure 1.2). So, we can only imagine how many smart devices there are in the world right at this time.

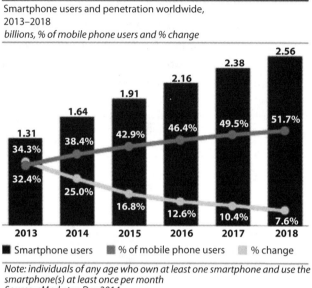

Smartphone users and penetration worldwide, 2013–2018
billions, % of mobile phone users and % change

Note: individuals of any age who own at least one smartphone and use the smartphone(s) at least once per month
Source: eMarketer, Dec 2014
182903   www.eMarketer.com

Figure 1.1   Growth of worldwide users of smart devices.

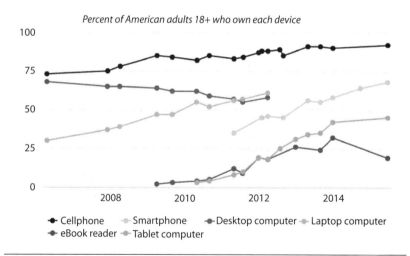

Figure 1.2   Ownership of different smart devices by American adults (Pew Research Center).

2

OWNERSHIP OF DEVICES

2.1 Corporate Owned versus Bring Your Own Device versus Company Owned, Personally Enabled

Now that we know what a smart device is, we will look at how these devices are introduced into the corporation. In the current computing environment, a smart device, as discussed in Chapter 1, is a small portable computer. Because it is a computer, organizations discovered that they can provide information quicker to their clients and customers by allowing their employees to use smart devices to connect to the corporate network and access data. Imagine that you are a salesperson with a prospective client. You realize that you will gain a new client if you can only show them what your company is about to introduce to the market that will solve their problem. Luckily, you have your connected iPad or Surface Pro. You whip out your tablet, connect to your corporate network, and demo the new widget to the prospective client. Voila! You have a new client just because you did not have to drive or fly back to your office so that you can get some pictures and brochures that you can share with the client.

The ability to delegate decision making and information where you need it is one of the reasons for the introduction of smart devices within the corporate environment. You can reach somebody with an email or text the person so that they have the requisite information on their smart device. It is the age of information where you need it. However, the introduction of smart devices into the corporate environment has not been a simple and easy road.

Corporations are just beginning to get a handle on how to manage their network perimeter, and here come smart devices that will poke holes into their network perimeter. Needless to say, smart devices were not readily accepted by some companies, especially information

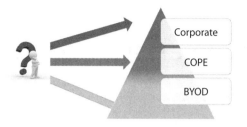

Figure 2.1   Three types of ownership of corporate smart devices.

technology (IT), because there is a cost. The cost is not just money. For the trailblazers that accepted the new technology, they realized that they have to prepare the IT environment for smart devices. They enhanced their virtual private network (VPN), if they had one, or introduced one, if they did not. They enhanced their access control, and those corporations that did not prepare suffered the consequences. The three ways corporations introduce smart devices into their organizations are (1) through corporate ownership of the smart devices, (2) through user-owned devices, otherwise known as bring your own device (BYOD), or through a recent hybrid called company owned, personally enabled (COPE) (Figure 2.1).

2.1.1 Corporate-Owned Devices

The smart devices' introduction for trailblazing companies is mainly the organization issuing a company-owned smart device to the employees. Usually, the organization thinks that a particular group of employees using the smart device will benefit the company. Think back to the BlackBerry era, and you will find the same trend where organizations issued a BlackBerry to employees whom they think will use it to the benefit of the company. Not everybody was immediately issued a BlackBerry. Of course not. There is a cost that is associated with that. The advantage of a company-issued smart device is that the company can control how these smart devices connect to their IT environment. The company can also control what applications can run on the smart device. Take BlackBerry for example; it is successful in the corporate world because the organization has more control of how the employee connected to the corporate network and what information is served to the employee. In the early days, the information from BlackBerry was mainly your email and your calendar. The many reasons for corporate-owned and company-issued smart devices are listed as follows and discussed in detail in the subsequent paragraphs:

- Standardization
- Compliance
- Control and information security
- Data ownership
- Bulk savings
- Corporate support

Standardization: Smart device technology is changing so fast, and the underlying operating systems, such as iOS, Android, and Windows, are changing much faster. If you have an Apple iOS device, you will know that, every time you turn around, Apple is introducing an iOS upgrade or patch. On the Android side, there were even more differences between versions. Android 2.1 is very different from Android 3.0, which is different from Android 5.0. To stabilize the introduction of technology, organizations issued these smart devices to their employees. This, of course, meant that the control of what technology is introduced and supported by IT remains with IT. In a sense, IT wanted it that way so that they can prescribe what happens with smart devices within the organization. In a way, it was meant to help the organization gradually adjust to change and properly manage the expenses that are associated with its change. For other IT groups, it was an aversion to change, and the fear of the loss of control that was the driver for corporate-issued smart devices. Yet, for some, the driver was the protection of sensitive information.

Compliance: For organizations that handled sensitive information, and are required by law to protect sensitive information, compliance was the driver for issuing corporate-owned smart devices. It is easier for these companies to issue preconfigured company smart devices to their employees. In doing so, they can attest to these smart devices being compliant to regulations and standards. Take, for example, a hospital that handles personal medical records, as well as personal information including credit card information; it is much easier for the hospital to issue a preconfigured and protected tablet to the doctors and nurses to use to view medical records. So hospitals issued tablets to nurses' stations that are configured not to display patient information if the smart device is activated beyond certain hospital boundaries. Because of this, hospitals are able to configure smart devices that can operate within certain hospital wards when operated by employees with the proper credentials. The device will automatically shut down when the device is taken outside the authorized working area. For these reasons, these companies absorbed the cost of issuing smart devices to their employees.

Control and information security: With the newer smart devices, there are a lot of apps available to the individual and the organizations. Go to Apple's iTunes, Google's Play Store, or Microsoft's Store, and you will find thousands of apps that range from entertainment to productivity and everything in between. Some of these apps may also contain malware and can be used to break into a company's network if they are vulnerable. Moreover, some organizations only want to provide to their employees those apps that can help with productivity and not the apps that may deter them from performing their job. With the introduction of mobile device management (MDM) systems, it became easier for organizations to easily define a whitelist of allowed applications that they push out to the company-owned devices. With MDM systems, organizations can specifically define unwanted apps in a blacklist or approved applications in a whitelist. Organizations can easily prescribe what apps are allowed on their own devices. If the organization handles sensitive information, it is important for them to protect the information by issuing their own smart devices to their employees and defining a whitelist or blacklist on the device, which the organization cannot do on a device that is owned by the employee. For these reasons, organizations choose to issue corporate-owned smart devices to their employees.

To better manage and secure the devices and protect their IT environment, organizations develop security policies, usually through their MDM solution, that are pushed to the devices. These policies include the implementation of corporate password policies on the devices, the definition of VPN connectivity, the verification of the existence of a malware protect solution, a firewall, etc. These policy configurations can determine what can be run on the device and who can run what app.

Data ownership: The ownership of data and information is another reason why companies choose to issue smart devices to their employees. Usually, these companies will have a corporate policy that informs the employees that all their work on company-owned devices belongs to the organization. Any ideas or designs created by the employee on a corporate-owned device is, in effect, the organization's property. With a signed document issued to the employees as part of their employment or issuing a smart device, the organization can now lay claim to the next best thing that can come from any of its employees. Some organizations see smart devices as a venue for the collection of ideas. While they encourage the employees to have these ideas and record them on the company-provided smart devices, these organizations also know that the information contained in these smart devices is a gold mine of answers to the question, "What is next for our company?"

Bulk savings: Another reason for corporate-owned devices is purely based on the bottom line and savings. In the article in *Financial Post*, "Beyond BYOD: Welcome to the Era of Corporate Owned, Personally Enabled (COPE) Devices," Lynn Greiner suggests that another reason for corporate ownership is finance. Corporate ownership means that the organization foots the bill and, as such, can negotiate very good prices for the devices and the service from the network providers. The contract amount for devices and services are always less than the list price and the price that a single individual can negotiate. This saves a lot of money for the organization.

2.1.2 BYOD

The other path taken by some companies was to allow employees to use their personal devices to connect to corporate network and data. This is aptly called bring your own device. Companies develop acceptable use policies for allowing employees to connect their respective devices to the corporate network and data. These policies specify the dos and don'ts of using a personal device on the corporate IT infrastructure. The policies contain requirements such as the following:

- Password, as defined by the organization
- Malware program for antivirus and firewall
- Encryption of data at rest and in motion
- Agreement that an organization can wipe the personal device if the organization deems it necessary
- Approved application list and disapproved application list

Some organizations require that the devices used by the employees support the ability to create a separate container for the organization that is protected and secure and does not intermingle corporate data with personal data. This intermingling of corporate and personal data on a smart device is one of the reasons that some organizations choose to own the device. Available MDM solutions provide this ability to separate corporate and personal data. Corporate data may include emails, management reports, client information, market analysis, etc., that are important to the corporation. Smart devices also contain personal information such as family and friends' names, numbers, addresses, and birthdays. It may also contain personal financial information or passwords to personal files. For the employee, these two types of data are needed to function in the modern-day world. So why do some organizations allow BYOD and others do not? The reasons why one company will allow BYOD and the other will not are listed as follows and discussed in detail consequently:

- Cost reduction
- Freedom of choice
- Increased productivity
- Abstraction of data
- Virtualization of space

Cost reduction: One of the reasons for BYOD is cost. Who bears the cost of smart devices in the organization? Smart devices are not cheap. Smart devices range in price from $300 to over $2,000. The lowest-priced Apple watch goes for about $349, a 16-GB iPad Air is listed for $499, a Samsung Galaxy 6 Edge goes for about $900, and a fully configured Surface Pro 3 is listed for about $2,000. Considering the price of the devices, as well as the cost of cell phone service from telephone companies, some companies choose to shift this cost to the employees and assume the risks that are associated with BYOD. Some of the risks are discussed in Section 2.1. One of those risks is the loss of control. With BYOD, the company does not really have a say as to what the employee can install or not install on the device. There are many malwares available that can infect the smart device and, from there, into the corporate network. Hackers are also looking at infiltrating the corporate network by hacking the smart device. Once the smart device is hacked, the intruder can tunnel into the corporate network. In addition, the hacker can obtain a lot of valuable information from the compromised smart device itself. In addition to the initial cost of the device, there is a replacement cost should the device be damaged or lost. So, in spite of the risks with BYOD, some organizations are willing to use BYOD as their enterprise smart device management approach.

With changes in the business environment, modern-day business relies on contractors. This trend is expected to continue to rise. A CareerBuilder hiring survey[*] suggests that 46% of employers plan to increase the use of contractors and other temporary workers. TechRepublic[†] suggests that this increase in hiring temporary workers is another reason why the organizations are moving to BYOD because the organizations do not see a need for absorbing the cost for providing smart devices to contractors.

BYOD reduces the time and effort that are expended in managing smart devices. With BYOD, the organization does not need to purchase an inventory management system to track the devices. The organization does not need to incur an additional cost in the management and tracking of these devices. If the device is lost, the organization will not expend any money or time in tracking the device. They can just remotely wipe the device or disconnect it from the network. At the end of the device's life, the organization does not need to bother about when to refresh their employees' smart devices and spend time and money to prepare the old devices for disposal. If implemented properly, company-issued devices are more likely to have company data stored on the device because there is no compartmentalization of personal and corporate spaces on the device. These costs are borne by the employees and the employees only.

Freedom of choice: The employees' freedom to choose a device of their liking is another reason for BYOD. In the current market,

---

[*] From the Career Builder Website: http://www.careerbuilder.com/share/aboutus/pressreleasesdetail.aspx?sd=1/1/2015&id=pr860&ed=12/31/2015.

[†] From the TechRepublic Website: http://www.techrepublic.com/article/5-reasons-why-byod-survived-2014-and-will-prosper-in-2015/.

there are a myriad of smart devices available. There are many designs from various companies. Even though the number of smart device manufacturers has reduced, the number of designs and the types of devices keep increasing. We initially had smartphones; then came tablets; and now we have added smart watches. As technology keeps on advancing, more uses will be identified, and more devices will be introduced. At the end of the day, the Internet of things will have its own impact on our definition of smart devices. Because companies recognize that people have different tastes, they are willing to allow their employees to be themselves and use the device that makes them happy.

Increased productivity: Another reason why some organizations move toward BYOD is an increase in employee productivity. By allowing employees to connect to corporate infrastructure with their personal smart devices, the organization expands the work environment and the working hours without saddling employees with another smart device to carry around. Remember the old days when employees issued beepers to some employees, and the employees wore a beeper and a cell phone all at the same time. It was the geeks' fashion statement. Then, the beepers went away. By allowing the employee to use their personal devices, they can reply to emails, check the project status, connect to clients, review reports, etc. In other words, they can continue to work even when they are at home or at the golf course. The organization gains because of this increased productivity with an additional cost to the organization. BYOD allows employees to work anywhere and at any time.

Abstraction of data: The advent of cloud computing has also pushed BYOD for some organizations. With many organizations moving data into the cloud, employees can then access the information from the cloud without touching the organization's internal IT infrastructure. It can be argued that the cloud is an extension of the internal network, but the information resides in an infrastructure that is not managed by the organization. So the organization can offload that information that is intended for the employees to access the cloud. Should anything happen to the employees' device, they can wipe it and/or disconnect it from the data in the cloud.

Virtualization of space: BYOD allows the organization to virtualize the organization's environment on the smart device. When the employee connects to the corporate network, a virtual environment is created with only the apps that are allowed by the organization. This virtualization separates the personal environment from the corporate environment. When the employee finishes work on the corporate virtualized compartment, the corporate section is closed, and no data are left behind because it will not allow data to be stored on the smart device.

2.1.3 COPE

Realizing that corporate ownership is one extreme that could be very expensive, and BYOD is another extreme with inherent security risks if not properly managed, organizations looked for another method that is possibly a hybrid between corporate ownership and BYOD (Figure 2.2). They found it.

The new hybrid combines some of the advantages of corporate ownership with that of BYOD. This new hybrid is called corporate owned, personally enabled. COPE gives device ownership still to the organizations, allowing users to personally configure the device with what they want so that the user has the same BYOD feel. COPE has its incentives for the organization and advantages for the employees. COPE tries to balance the organization's need for reduced risk, compliance, the control of their infrastructure, and support with the employees' need for choice. COPE gives both the organization and the employees almost everything that they want.

How does COPE work? The organization can determine the acceptable devices that they are willing to support. The organization can also negotiate the device prices for the acceptable devices from

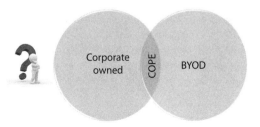

Figure 2.2 Corporate owned, personally enabled.

various providers. The organization can also identify an acceptable mobile service available for the employees from various carriers. The employee then selects a device from the list and installs both their personal apps and the organization's container and apps. The employee can connect their personal email, as well as the organization's email. Both the organization and the employee enjoy the advantages that are provided by COPE.

2.1.3.1 Advantages of COPE

COPE benefits both the organization and the employees. The organization gets the advantages of the consumerization of smart devices. In essence, it allows the employees to personalize their *company-issued* smart devices. The organization reduces cost by pooling minutes and allowing employees to use minutes from the pool. The negotiated services save both the organization and the employee some money. The employee also gets a company-negotiated price for the devices as they select the device of their liking. So the organizations reduce cost and maintain the control of the device vendors and carriers, while the employees enjoy their freedom to choose. As result, productivity is increased. Figure 2.3 shows the key characteristics of the three types of ownership.

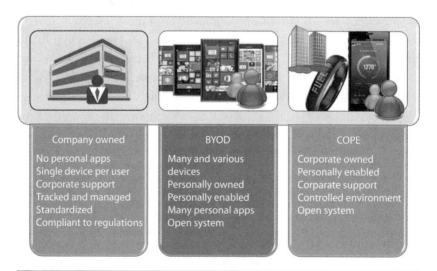

Company owned	BYOD	COPE
No personal apps	Many and various	Corporate owned
Single device per user	devices	Personally enabled
Corporate support	Personally owned	Corparate support
Tracked and managed	Personally enabled	Controlled environment
Standardized	Many personal apps	Open system
Compliant to regulations	Open system	

Figure 2.3   Key characteristics of three types of ownership.

3

DATA TYPES

3.1 Introduction

Do you ever wonder how, when you move into a new house, you have less stuff, especially if you are single or just married and without kids? You have fewer things initially, but then you start collecting *stuff* from everywhere. Then, the kids start coming, and you realize that you need more stuff for the kids. The kids get stuff from everywhere, especially from grandparents. Very soon, you will realize that your house is too small, and it is time to look for a bigger house. The same cycle happens with computers and now with mobile devices. We buy that mobile device with a *gazillion* memory and space thinking that we have all we need for a lifetime, but we start filling it up. In a way, smart devices affect and have changed our behavior toward them.

3.2 Email-Driven Era

So how do we fill up our smart devices? Where does the stuff we put in the device come from? In this chapter, we will examine the types of data that are stored in the smart device and the sources of such data. The device owner is one source of the data that are stored in the smart device, as well as app vendors.

Recall the short history of smart devices that we gave in Chapters 1 and 2 and how we moved from using the landline phone to make calls to the BlackBerry era. With the introduction of BlackBerry and the other smart devices of that era, the smart device became our connection to corporate and personal emails. All the emails we receive are stored on the device, both work and personal emails. At this point, we started to see the introduction of rudimentary apps like email. This, of course, meant that we needed some space to store all this information. Many of us do not believe in deleting emails and used the smart device as our email storage. Our smart device keeps us connected to the office and everything happening around us. It also contains our contacts. Instead of the Rolodex, all the contact information can be stored in the smart device. This makes it easier to send an email or call a person using the smart device without having to carry the Rolodex. How simple and how wonderful!

Small personal apps, such as music and video players, became a part of the smart device. Some of us purchased applications that will convert our CDs into MP3 music, and then we download our MP3 music to the device by connecting the smart device to our computer and syncing the two. The inclusion of our music and video library meant that additional space is required to store all our data. Advancements in technology, of course, gave us small form factor drives such as the solid-state drive and, as such, the storage space in smart devices increased. The more we were able to do with our smart devices, the more we demanded of them, and the smart device manufacturers obliged us. Or is it the other way around?

3.3 Data on Smart Device

As smart device technology improved and the manufacturers kept impressing us with newer and better smart devices, a new era began. With faster processing power and increased memory and storage, we realized that smart devices can do many of the things that we do on our laptops and desktops. But where are the apps? We need the apps to take our work, music, movies, and games with us anywhere we went. Apple and Google encouraged developers to create applications for Apple and Android devices. We can now get applications for work and play and install them in our device and take the device anywhere we go. Therein lies the appeal of the smart device.

3.3.1 Entertainment

With developers creating apps for everything, we have applications from Web browsers to games. Parents now have a new portable entertainment device for the kids. Gone is the day of "Are we there yet?" Any parent who has taken their kids on a long trip before the advent of smart devices can definitely relate to this: the incessant nagging from kids who are tired of sitting in the same spot for the long duration of a car ride. The apps stored in the smart devices provided hours and hours of entertainment for the kids on those long trips and kept them entertained whenever they got bored.

The smart device also serves as a storage for the books that we like to read and those that we have to read. When your favorite author publishes a new book, you can immediately purchase that on Amazon and download it on your Kindle reader or any other smart device that supports the Kindle app. When you need a book that deals with a topic that you want to learn, you can immediately download that from Amazon, Apple, or Android into your device and read it. Access to information and knowledge is much closer when needed.

3.3.2 Streaming

Our society, especially the younger generation, is the *I-need-it-now* generation. We need our music now, and we need our video now. We need it now quicker and faster. Most people purchase music from online providers such as iTunes, Google, or Amazon. We need our videos from iTunes, Google, Amazon, Netflix, Hulu, etc., now. To get what is needed without delay, providers have given us the ability to stream our music or video. The streamed content is partly stored on the smart device. The ability to stream content is facilitated by cell phone providers who continually provide increased bandwidth, although at a price. The need to get what we want now is also changing the way that the society wants to be entertained. Gone are the days when the only way to listen to a favorite radio station is through a radio and within the area where the radio station broadcasts its signal. Now, your favorite radio station can be accessed through the smart device from anywhere around the world. We are now, willingly or otherwise, able to store our habits on the smart device.

3.3.3 Office Work

The apps published include the apps that can make any place an office. These applications are office-related apps that provided things such as word processing, spreadsheets, and presentation apps. Now, smart device owners can create or edit documents wherever they are. It now extends the concept of an office by allowing the smart device user to work on documents that will normally require being at the office or at a desktop/laptop.

3.3.4 Geolocation

With the introduction of Global Positioning System (GPS) apps, geolocation data are now stored in smart devices. As you drive around in your car while talking on your smartphone, the smartphone changes from one cell tower to another as you come into the cell tower's area (Figure 3.1). This information is recorded in the smart device. Have you ever heard of Waze? It is a GPS and a social media app available on both Android and Apple devices. Not only is it a wonderful app, but it also records the routes that you are traveling, your friends whom you can communicate with when on Waze, your contact information, and a lot of other very good and, sometimes, personal information. When your smart device connects to a wireless network, this location information is also stored in the smart device. When you take a picture with your smart device, the pictures are tagged with geolocation information. The chat apps on smart devices also provide geolocation information. The geolocation information stored in the smart device is wonderful and provides information to smart device owners,

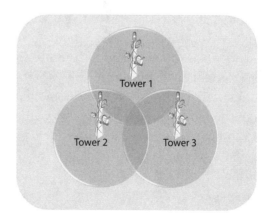

Figure 3.1   Cell phone towers.

and, at the same time, geolocation data may have security and legal implications.

The geolocation information in a smart device is a source of information to both hackers and law enforcement. Imagine that your phone is stolen or hacked; now, the hacker knows about all your contacts. The hacker can also tell where you have been and who you have communicated with and when. The same goes for law enforcement officers who can use the information recorded on the smartphone as a source of crucial information in an investigation. For the people who perform banking transactions with their smart device, the hacker can also obtain your banking information. The diagram in Figure 3.1 shows three cell phone towers with their coverage areas. As the cell phone user travels from the Tower 1 area to the Tower 2 area, Tower 1 hands over the call to Tower 2 without the caller knowing. This information is logged and time-stamped.

Imagine that you have a legal proceeding and were asked to turn over your smart device. Tom Brady of the New England Patriots comes to mind here. He was being investigated for the deflation of the football below the National Football League's specification and was asked to turn over his smartphone to the investigators. According to the report, Tom Brady cancelled his smartphone with the cell phone service provider and destroyed the smart device itself. It shows an understanding of the implications of somebody else looking at the data that are stored in your smart device. The police and the courts can obtain a great amount of information from the data stored in your smart device. For a computer forensic investigator, or any investigator for that matter, the data in smart devices are a gold mine.

Another aspect of geolocation is the hotspots that are provided by Internet service providers (ISPs). AT&T, Verizon, Time Warner, Comcast, etc., have their own respective hotspot networks around the country. This essentially means that anyone traveling around the country can be connected to the ISP's hotspot. This leaves traces of location due to the connection information. This information can be of benefit to an investigator who is interested in tracing the whereabouts of a device and the device owner. The ISP can also track the customer's movement by analyzing the same hotspot connection information.

3.3.5 Messages

The new generation tends to use texting more often than phone calls or emails to communicate. At work, texting has also increased as a means of communication. The messages sent from the smart device are stored in the device. Even when the user deletes the text messages, the messages are still there for anybody who is interested and with the know-how to retrieve the deleted data. The text messages are time-stamped and show who sent a message and when the message was sent. If you use apps such as Waze, the smart device will also store data on where the message was sent from. Many smart device users are oblivious to the fact that most texting apps are not configured to encrypt the text message. When the smart device is hacked or falls into unsavory hands, the text messages are in the clear, including those that are supposedly deleted.

Another aspect of texting data is that short message service is controlled by telcos. In many countries, telcos are government owned or controlled. As such, these foreign governments can gain access to your text information at will without any court permissions. There is no presumption of protection for the user. Imagine that you are a corporate user, and a partner in China or Iran texted you with some sensitive information, and you responded. This information is now readily available to the snoops at the foreign government through their access to the telcos. The text messages may also contain sensitive personal health information that should be protected and is a violation of US laws. Text data have many security and compliance ramifications for the company. Text messages include one-on-one smart device messages, Web-based messaging, call centers, and answering services.

3.3.6 Financial Information

Most financial institutions have an app for their customers for their personal banking and/or investments. Using a smart device, a person can check the balance on their account, pay bills, transfer funds from one account to another, buy and sell stocks, etc. All these financial institutions require an account in order to connect. The financial institution can even send an alert to the customer on the smart device when certain defined events occur.

3.4 The Age of the Internet of Things

Remember in Chapters 1 and 2 that we included the Internet of things in the definition of smart devices. It is hard not to notice that smart devices are now embedded in various things that we use daily. Smart devices are embedded in doors, gates, cars, home appliances, etc. Smart devices have the ability to lock and unlock the doors in our homes. In a gated community, you can open the gates to your community or house by selecting the app or dialing the number for your gate.

Car manufacturers now embed smart devices in the car that collect and store information about your car so that, when you go for services, the technician can quickly diagnose the problem. Not that it has made going to the car repair shop any cheaper. However, the technician has a lot of information to repair your car. Subscribers to General Motors' (GM's) OnStar get monthly reports from GM on the data collected by the smart device in their vehicles and sent to GM. The OnStar report includes the engine, transmission, emission system, antilock brake, oil levels, tire pressure, mileage history, etc.

Late-model cars can also record your driving habits. Some newer-model cars can detect when a driver is falling asleep and take over the driving. Some will apply brakes when the driver gets too close to the vehicle in front. Yet others will try to avoid collision in places like an intersection or when changing lanes on a highway. While these make life easier for the driver, these devices collect a great amount of data about the vehicle and the driver.

The collected vehicle data are of interest not only to the car manufacturers but also to the insurance companies. The Government Employees Insurance Company advertised that it will lower its subscriber's insurance if the subscribers will plug in a smart device in their car that collects information on the driver's driving habits. It will detect and store the driver's speed with the legal speed limit. It will also collect data on the frequency of driving, as well as any other information that it obtains from integration with the car's computer. So the car is no longer your private sanctuary because all the data collected by the smart devices in the car can provide information to third parties, which many not be to the driver's advantage.

3.4.1 Monitoring and Control

Another type of data that make its way to smart devices falls under the monitoring and control category. Closed-circuit cameras were a thing for businesses that want to monitor their environment. Now, high-definition cameras are available to monitor homes as well. The video data collected by these cameras can be sent to the smart device through an app. You can be a thousand miles away and still monitor what is going on in your house.

Smart devices allow us to monitor not only our home and environment; they also allow us to monitor ourselves. Smart devices allow us to monitor our health. There are apps or devices, like Fitbit, that allow you to record your exercise habits. The number of steps you take per day is recorded, and the number of miles that you are running is recorded. Some of the apps allow the user to record their eating habits as well so that the users can find a balance between what they eat, how much they eat, and how much they need to exercise. These data are stored in the smart device and can be of interest to healthcare providers and insurance companies.

Using a smart device, it is possible to control various aspects of your environment. Smart devices can collect data about the temperature in your home and allow you to adjust the temperature even when you are not at home. The television can now be controlled with a smart device. Not only can you control the TV with the smart device; it can also store the frequently watched TV stations.

3.5 The Age of Corporate Connectivity

One of the benefits provided by smart devices is mobility. With mobility, employees realized that smart devices can provide them with access to corporate data wherever they are and at whatever time. The ability to respond quickly became paramount for companies. As such, organizations began to grant access to corporate networks, systems, and data to their employees. Not only are employees granted access to data themselves, but organizations also began to develop their own private apps. These apps format data to be presented to the employees. At present, a salesperson can run an app on his or her smart device and pull product or customer information from the corporate SAP, Oracle, or SalesForce.com. It allows the salesperson to make that last pitch to convince a potential buyer. In other to satisfy corporate needs, corporate data are finding their way into smart devices. There are many types of corporate data that can find their way into a smart device, and, in some cases, some of the data should not make their way into the smart devices.

3.5.1 Network Connectivity

The ability to access corporate data is made possible through corporate connectivity. Corporate networks are made of wired and wireless networks. Smart devices, for the most part, use Wi-fi to connect to a corporate network. In some organizations, a separate virtual local area network (VLAN) is created for smart devices. This access through a segregated network provides a layer of security for the organization and allows the organization to properly authenticate the user and the device before access is granted to any internal data or application (see Figure 3.2). The connection data are stored on the smart device so that the smart device

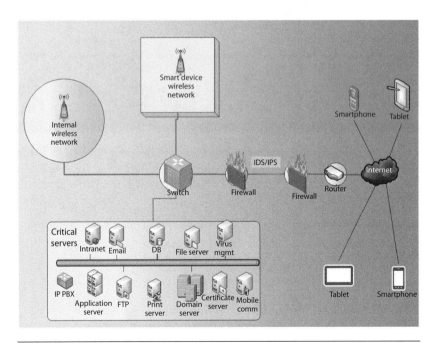

Figure 3.2   Corporate infrastructure with a segregated Wi-fi VLAN for smart devices. DB, data base; FTP, file transfer protocol; IP, internet protocol; PBX, private branch exchange.

can automatically connect when in range or when specifically activated by the user. Once connected to the corporate network, the user has access to apps and data that are available to the user and the device.

3.5.2 Physical Access Key Code

One of the types of corporate data that are stored on the smart device is access codes for the doors to the offices. Instead of spending additional money in making and tracking key cards, organizations are using a smart device–enabled lock-and-key system to grant access to the building. The employee's smart device is granted access to the building door, and a code is sent to the device. The code determines what doors the employee is allowed to open. The employee uses the app in the smart device to open the door. It saves the organization some money in managing and tracking key cards. However, should the employee lose his or her smart device, the organization will activate their incidence response so that the key code and any other organization data will be wiped from the smart device.

3.5.3 Employee Information

Every employee in an organization has a certain level of access to, at least, their own employee data. For the employees who deal with employee data, they have access to the data for many, if not all, of the organization's employees. At present, systems are now mobile enabled so that human resources can work from anywhere. Since these mobile devices access employee data, these data are downloaded on the device. Some of the information about the employee may be sensitive, but the downloaded data are now in the smart device even after the app is closed. A dedicated intruder can scrub the smart device to obtain the necessary information. This will have implications for things such as Health Insurance Portability and Accountability Act compliance.

3.5.4 Customer and Business Partner Information

Companies are doing business to sell their products to the customers. To produce their product, the company may buy materials and parts from various vendors. For most companies, customer information and vendor information are sensitive and very much protected. Employees who have access to customers' or third-party vendors' information can also access that information when they are granted access on a smart device. Customer information may have credit card information, and, as this is viewed by the employee, that data are downloaded to the employee's smart device.

In addition, businesses are using smart devices attached to smartphones to accept credit card payments from customers. The smart device, through the smartphone, verifies the credit card before allowing the transaction to be completed. Square, from Square, Inc., is a very good example. In this case, two smart devices are used in the transaction. While Square makes credit card transactions more accessible, especially to small businesses, it has bigger ramifications for the Payment Card Industry (PCI) compliance for some vendors.

In addition to Square, there are Apple Pay, CurrentC, Google Pay, and the yet-to-be-launched Samsung Pay. These companies and their products use the smartphone as a financial instrument. Your smartphone is like a debit or credit card. It can be used to purchase anything wherever these *near* currencies are used. Your smart device will then need to be protected just like your credit card. Not only does the smart device owner have to protect and safeguard the smartphone; the company also has to protect the information obtained from these smartphone transactions. There are government and PCI compliance ramifications should a hacker break into these sites.

3.5.5 Product Information

Companies have products that they want to tell customers and potential customers about. These can be found in the company's product catalog or on their Website. On the other hand, there are products in research and development (R&D) that companies, in most cases, do not want to talk about. Car manufacturers will go to any length to hide and protect information about a new car or engine that they are developing. The idea is to gain competitive advantage. A lot of data are collected by the company during the development and testing of the new product, and this information is not something that the company wants disclosed to its competitors. However, access to the R&D information can be made available to the R&D employees through smart devices. As such, the employee can connect to the company network and download R&D product information on their tablet and review such information on the smart device. That data are now on the smart device, and that increases the risk of disclosure.

3.6 The Age of Repositories

With the many apps being developed for Apple and Android devices, there was a need for a repository for all the things that are loaded into the smart device. Here come Apple's iTunes, Google's Play Store, Amazon, etc. These companies' solutions provided marketplaces where people can purchase new games, music, books, and any apps that are published on the marketplace. The repositories stored data on the smart devices, as well as offline. In most cases, the smart device downloads all purchased content to your computer and, from there, synchronizes with the smart device.

For some companies, there was a need to create their own internal marketplace for all their supported apps. For companies that issue smart devices, this is a way for them to control the apps that are available to their employees and reduce the risks that are associated with smart devices. The marketplace information and the connection to the marketplace are maintained on the smart device.

Initially, the repositories used local storage space on the user's computer. For an example, Apple's iTunes uses storage space on the user's local computer. The user's music, video, photos, apps, etc., are all stored on the local drive. The local storage also served as the backup location. The user can perform a backup of their Apple device to their local storage through iTunes' synchronization. This makes it possible for the user to restore their iPhone from the backup. For most repositories, the constraint was the local drive.

3.7 The Age of the Cloud

The constraint from local drive storage was addressed by Google and Amazon because the content that is purchased from them is stored for the user at Google's or Amazon's site. The cloud storage for smart devices was born. With the advent of cloud computing applications (Figure 3.3), systems and storage are moved to the cloud and thereby

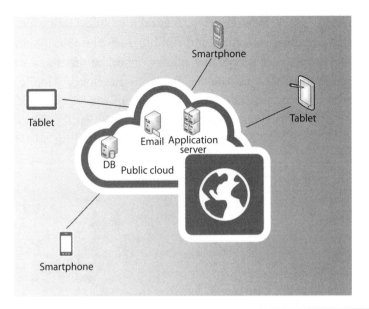

Figure 3.3 High-level cloud architecture.

provide access to the smart device user from anywhere. The smart device user is no longer tied to the storage on the local computer but can move all the content on the smart device to the cloud.

The smart device owner can perform backups to the cloud and restore from the cloud. Synchronization occurs between the smart device and the cloud. In iTunes, the user can synchronize to the cloud, and all purchased content is stored in Apple's iCloud. With Amazon, a Kindle user automatically connects to their content on Amazon once authentication has been established. Amazon then allows the user to download the content that he or she wants to the Kindle or any smart device running the Kindle app.

The advantage of a cloud content for the smart device is that it adds to the mobility of smart devices. Smart devices can connect to the cloud content anywhere as long as there is an Internet connection. The user can either access the content in the cloud or download the content to a smart device. The cloud also made mobile Web computing possible. With mobile Web computing, the smart device can run Web apps that are cloud based. This is made possible with the advent of HTML 5. It is no longer only those apps that are developed for that particular smart device. Instead, cloud-based Web apps are developed so that they can run across mobile platforms. This is of interest to corporations that want to develop their own mobile applications. This way, they can develop it once and run it across multiple mobile platforms. Mobile cloud computing allows organizations to run robust applications on the smart device through the cloud. Mobile cloud computing is the direction that many organizations are taking in other to provide the same applications across all smart device platforms and control the access and security for the applications.

4

Uses and Benefits of Smart Devices

4.1 Introduction

The general worldwide acceptance of smart devices has made them one of the most ubiquitous technologies. They can be found in every industry including automotive, financial, retail, manufacturing, oil and gas, banking, and government agencies. They can be found among all walks of life: schoolteachers, students, salespeople, warehouse workers, distribution workers, oil rig tool pushers, photographers, etc. Like clockwork, smart device manufacturers such as Apple and Samsung seem to find new uses, sometimes driven by users, and new designs to keep the user always interested. Between four and six months, a new device will be introduced to the market, only to be usurped by a faster, smarter, and sleeker device from a competitor. The question, then, is how are we using these smart devices, and what are their benefits that keep us interested?

4.2 Anywhere Communication

Smart devices have changed how we communicate. Do you remember the old days when the best way to communicate was by using corded telephones? Many retail stores made a lot of money selling 30- and 50-ft. cords so that, when you needed some privacy, you could take the phone into a room and close the door behind you. If you needed to contact somebody while you were traveling, you had to find the nearest pay phone. Smart devices have changed all that. People currently rely on their smart devices for their communication. According to

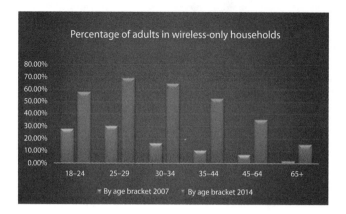

Figure 4.1   Pew Research Center study on wireless only households.

the Pew Research Center* research (Figure 4.1), published in January 2015, 43% of US adults do not have any corded phones but only have smartphones. This is a big jump from 2008 when 25% of US adults did not have corded phones and only had smartphones. This trend will probably continue until landlines go the way of the dinosaurs.

The ability to communicate with anybody from anywhere is one of the biggest advantages of smart devices. Smart devices make it possible for us to communicate with others while shopping, playing, on vacation, etc. It does not matter what we are doing or where we are; we can communicate with others in many different ways. We can talk to, exchange text messages with, or email a person. With the addition of apps like Twitter and Instagram, a smart device user can post messages to a group of people all at the same time. If you are on vacation, you can take pictures with a smartphone, and smartphones have the ability to keep a history of your vacation in a chronological fashion so that your friends and family can follow you on your vacation and virtually be there with you. Smart devices have made the ability to communicate instant, quick, and easy.

The ability to communicate from anywhere at any time provides a sense of safety and security to the user. Let us say that you have a flat tire in the middle of nowhere. You pick up your smartphone and call the nearest tow truck or roadside assistance for rescue. While you are

---

* From the Pew Research Center Website: http://www.pewresearch.org.

waiting for the assistance to arrive, you can listen to music, watch a video or a movie, and/or play a game.

The ability to communicate with people anywhere and at any time has also made smart devices an important business tool. Smart devices provide businesses the ability to reach their customers quickly and, as such, reduces the time to market. A salesperson can quickly pull data from corporate systems and present the latest information to a client. A company can blast a new widget to its customers on their smart devices. Take, for example, the grocery business. Grocery retailers, like other retailers, create their own app, which the shoppers can download on their smart devices. When a product of interest is discounted, the shopper is notified immediately. Also, at the store, the shopper can identify the weekly or daily sales from the retailer. This bypasses the old paper advertisement channel and allows the retailer to advertise directly to the shopper and thereby saves the grocery retailer advertisement money.

4.3 Entertainment

The main use of small devices is for entertainment. Log in to iTunes, Google Play Store, or Amazon, and you will find thousands of entertainment uses for smart devices. During the vinyl record days, we purchased our music by going to the music store and riffling through many vinyl records in your type of music category, looking for an album or a single that was just released or that you heard and liked. Going to the music store was a part of the process and entertainment. Sometimes, you will go with some friends making it a group enjoyment. After returning home from the music store, you turn on your player and put the album on, making sure that the needle is in good shape. Then, you hear that scratchy beginning of all vinyl before the first song starts. You were in heaven.

Smart devices have changed that. The songs are now digital, and so are the albums. The music store has been replaced by virtual cloud stores such as iTunes and Google Play Store. To purchase a song, the buyer signs in to their favorite digital music store and searches for the song or album that he or she wants. Once purchased, the song is downloaded into the smart device, and the buyer can go anywhere and listen to the music. No scratchy sound. Nothing but crisp, clean digital music.

But songs and digital albums are not the only things that you can purchase from these virtual cloud music stores. You can also buy various types of video games and books from these stores. The old vinyl music stores did not have any video games, since video games, such as Atari, came out later and were sold by other stores. The video games provide hours of entertainment for the users. These days, when a family prepares for a long-distance travel, either by airplane or by car, a part of the preparation is making sure that everybody has downloaded the music, games, and books that they will need for the duration of the travel. Imagine traveling with a nine-year-old boy on a road trip, and you downloaded NBA games, NFL games, and a car racing game on a tablet for him. He will be glued to these games all throughout the journey, and, when he gets tired of the games, he can start watching a movie on the smart device. It makes the journey more enjoyable, and, if you are driving, you will be spared the "Are we there yet?" questions.

Smart devices have also changed the way that we listen to radios and our favorite radio stations. It used to be that, when you travelled out of your local area, you would not be able to listen to your favorite radio station. That has all changed. Because of smart devices, a new type of radio is available. These include iHeartRadio, Pandora, Apple Music, etc. These cloud radio stations include some of the same local stations and syndicated programs. Local radio stations also broadcast on the Internet, and, with a smart device, individuals can listen to their favorite radio station.

Smart devices have consolidated our entertainment and, at the same time, made them portable. We can take our music anywhere. We can sit at the airport and watch a movie on our smart device while we wait for that delayed flight. We can read a book on the flight while we are listening to music, all on the same device. Our entertainment is at our fingertips, anywhere and at any time.

4.4 Financial Instrument

First, it was trade by barter where we exchanged goods for goods. Then, we introduced money, and we paid with gold and silver. Then came paper currency and credit cards, and now we have digital money. Smart devices immediately became impactful after the introduction of digital money because banks and other financial institutions developed apps that allow people to check the balance on their account from anywhere. It provided access to our account quickly and easily. But this was only the beginning.

At present, smart devices have gone beyond checking the balance on your account to becoming a financial instrument. Apple has the Apple Pay, and there is the Square, and now there is Samsung Pay, which even has the image of your credit card.

4.4.1 Apple Pay

Apple Pay, Apple's payment technology, is available as a standard feature with iPhone 6 and up and Apple Watch (Figure 4.2). The idea

Figure 4.2   Apple Pay—iPhone and Watch.

behind Apple Pay, and all other smart device payment technologies, is to make payment and purchasing much easier. Instead of carrying a fat wallet, all your credit and debit cards are aggregated in the Passbook app. Apple uses near-field communication (NFC), a Secure Element chip, which stores encrypted payment information, and Touch ID for the base technology for communication.

The user stores credit card and debit card information in the Passbook. The user pays for purchases by placing the Apple smart device close to the credit card terminal and selecting the card to use. This makes Touch ID to prompt the user to authenticate the payment transaction. Voila! You have paid for your purchase without bringing out your wallet and without an additional signature. Apple Pay creates a security code dynamically without providing payment card details to the retailer. American Express, MasterCard, Visa, and the major banks, such as Chase, Citibank, and Wells Fargo, already support Apple Pay.

4.4.2 Samsung Pay

Samsung Pay (Figure 4.3), just like Apple Pay, uses NFC technology to process payments at the tap-to-pay terminals, as well as other magnetic strip terminals that can be found at most retail stores. In the other uses of Samsung Pay, a Samsung Galaxy S6 edge+, a Galaxy S6 edge, a Galaxy S6 active, a Galaxy Note5, or a Galaxy S6 is required. Subscription to a cell phone carrier, such as AT&T, T-Mobile, Sprint Verizon, MetroPCS, Cricket, or US Cellular, is required for communicating with the financial institution. In addition, a credit or debit card from American Express, MasterCard, or Visa is a requirement. The credit or debit card must be provided by the Bank of America, Chase, Citibank, PNC, Synchrony, or US Bank.

There are three steps in using Samsung Pay:

1. Download and install Samsung Pay.
2. Configure Samsung Pay on the device.
3. Add payment cards.

Using Samsung Pay requires the user's fingerprint, which is securely stored during the configuration of Samsung Pay. By placing your finger on the home button and pressing the back of the device on the

Figure 4.3   Samsung Pay—available on smart device.

terminal, the payment transaction will be initiated. When completed, an Android notification is sent to the user confirming the merchant and the transaction.

4.4.3 Square Payment

At present, anybody can accept credit cards anywhere by using the Square payment device (Figure 4.4). Square payment is one of the first payment devices that process credit cards through a Square device that is attached to the smart device (Figure 4.5). Square, Inc. developed the Square Register device to allow individuals and merchants in the United States, Canada, and Japan to accept credit and debit card payment. The Square requires the Square Reader where the user swipes the credit card for processing. Unlike Apple Pay and

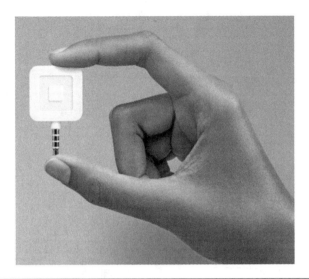

Figure 4.4 Square hardware—attaches to smart devices.

Figure 4.5 Users swipe credit card using the Square hardware.

Figure 4.6   Contactless use of Square device.

Samsung Pay, Square payment devices work with both Apple and Android smart devices.

With the release of Apple Pay, Google Pay, and Samsung that use NFC for communication, Square upgraded the Square Reader to accept contactless and chip-secured credit and debit cards (Figure 4.6). Square Reader uses Bluetooth for contactless operation or contact connection through the smart device's headphone jack. Apple is a user of the Square Contactless Readers. The Square app on Apple devices is designed to look like a cash register.

4.5 New Education Format

Take a quick look at modern-day education, and you immediately know that it is no longer your grandfather's education. Things have changed and drastically for that matter. In the 1970s and 1980s, we worked on mainframes. To register for a class, we went to the basketball arena because that was where each college and department set up for class registration. Students went from one department table to another and picked up a registration punch card for the class that they intended to take. Assuming that you wanted to take five three-hour classes for the semester, you have to first identify the five classes, go to the department's table, and obtain the punch card, which you then filled in with the help of the people working at the table. When you completed the registration of the punched card, you handed that back to the workers at the table before proceeding to the next table to register for the next class. The workers at the table gave you a paper to show that you registered for the class on the spot, but you would then receive another letter from the university showing all the classes for which you were formally registered. You then repeated this process for each of the five classes that you intended to attend. You planned to spend the whole day to register for your classes.

That's not all. Imagine the logistical nightmare of coordinating the process. Of course, you could not have 26,000 students in the basketball arena all at the same time. Instead, registration was by order. You had your time to register for classes. Miss it, and you would be late for registration and would be charged a late registration fee. In the late 1980s and 1990s, luckily, things had changed a great deal. We had desktops.

The use of smart devices in education reminds me of an old Virginia Slims cigarette advertisement that read, "You've come a long way, baby." We have definitely come a long way in education with smart devices. Education was improved with desktops and the Internet, but smart devices redefined the boundaries of the classroom and the scope of the curriculum (Figure 4.7).

Unlike the registration with punched cards on the mainframe in a basketball arena, modern-day students can register for classes from their smart devices from anywhere. The student's physical presence is not required to register for a class. Students can be on a bus, at a coffee shop, or at their favorite watering hole while they register for classes.

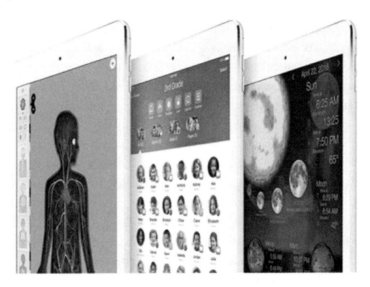

Figure 4.7   Use of smart devices for education.

The ease of use, in addition to portability, has made smart devices ubiquitous from a kindergarten classroom to a college classroom.

Smart devices provide immediate answers to students' questions and provide a wide access to information for the students. If a student does not understand a concept, they can immediately search the Internet from their smart device. This helps give the student a better understanding of the concept and increases their confidence in the education process. Take a student who is in an English class and sees a new word; the student can find the word on the Internet and hear the proper pronunciation of the word from the smart device. The smart device provides answers to the questions *how*, *what*, *where*, etc. Beyond the information related to classroom materials, the student is exposed to many other types of information on the Internet. While desktops and laptops brought education into the classrooms, smart devices put learning on the palm of students' hands.

Smart devices are a tool for teachers. In fact, they are a requirement for the school curriculum. Teachers prepare school materials and the subject matter based on how that material can be presented to the students on smart devices. Teachers prepare video materials that the students can watch on their smart devices. Smart devices engage the students in the learning process. Many schools have video libraries that students can log in to, where they can view the teacher's material. Through the smart device, the students gain access to school libraries, as well as the local city library. The student is encouraged to use voice recordings, photos, videos, and apps to create their own answers and stories. Teachers are expanding and extending their classrooms by incorporating other sources of information. For college students, some professors record their lectures and publish these lectures to the students. The college students can play these lecture videos at their convenience in their dorm rooms or apartments. The student has access to class materials 24/7 and more access to the professor beyond office hours.

Even the reading materials have changed. In the past, students had to carry huge hardback textbooks to each of their classes. If they forgot any of these books at home, the student would not be able to read or look up information. Things are different now with the use of smart devices. Textbooks are being digitized so that students can purchase digital copies of the books and just carry only the smart device

(Figure 4.8). Amazon Kindle has provided us a very convenient way to carry books and read at our own convenience anywhere and at any time.

Smart devices provide a ready communication medium between the school and the parents. If an emergency occurs at school, parents are notified on their smart devices. If a particular student has a problem, either health or behavior related, the school contacts the parents on their smart devices. Many teachers also send information to the parents about what the students learned or are expected to learn and what homeworks the students should be reading or solving.

Smart devices are going to continue to see more educational apps, and education is going to be an integral part of smart devices. Apple is about to release a new iOS (version 9.3) with multiuser support so that multiple students can use the same iPad, and each student's profile, apps, and music will be saved for them. Included in the same Apple iOS release is the *Classroom* app, which allows a teacher to control all iPads in the classroom, and the *Screen View*, which allows the teacher to view the student's screen. In addition, *Apple School Manager* is a hub for teachers to create course work, purchase apps and books, and track classroom iPads.

In addition, professional training schools have now seen the value of loading their training materials on smart devices. In the modern-day business, you have to keep improving, either because your profession

Figure 4.8   Electronic books are available on smart devices.

requires it or your certification requires it. The professional can then review these training materials at home or in the train as they travel to work or home. Professional certification training materials for professional certifications, such as CISSP*, have been created and loaded into tablets by many organizations. Even internal security awareness training for organizations is made available on smart devices.

4.6 Emergency Management

Smart devices are also used for safety in many communities. For example, take the communities in the tornado prone areas in the United States. When the weather conditions that can produce a tornado are observed, an emergency alert is sent to all the smartphones in that area. This gives the people who live in those communities enough time to seek safety. Another example is the Amber Alert. An Amber Alert is broadcast to all highway screens, as well as smart devices within an area, when a person is missing. The vehicle and description of the missing person or the abductor are broadcast on all smart devices in the area. This disseminates information quickly so that the missing person can be found quickly.

Visualization is an important aspect of emergency and crisis management. For management, incident/emergency managers, and the general populace, visualization is extremely helpful when there is a lot of confusion, uncertainty, and stress. During emergencies, people are usually not thinking straight, and having an app that is mobile and can present step-by-step instructions in a concise manner to be executed by the emergency/incident manager and his or her team is half the battle. The ability for top management to go to the same app on their tablet and view an up-to-the-second report as to how the emergency is being addressed goes a long way to reduce stress and provide the necessary resources that the emergency manager needs. Visualization is equally important and helpful for the general public or employees. Smart devices can be used to show employees the nearest exit or their assigned station during an emergency. If the app is

---

* CISSP is a certification for information security professionals that is provided by an organization called ISC². CISSP stands for Certified Information Systems Security Professional.

a part of the standard employee apps provided by the organization, the employee, the emergency manager can activate the app and direct people to the next course of action. This will go a long way in reducing panic. Securely Yours LLC developed a disaster recovery (DR) tool that helps organizations during a disaster. This app provides step-by-step instructions to the DR manager and his or her teams, as well as providing an up-to-the minute status report to management. It assigns the responsibilities for tasks and updates the task list as the tasks are completed.

In addition, smart devices can be used to perform a roll call during an emergency. A roll call is usually performed to account for human life. As a part of the emergency management process, a calling tree is developed, and a branch is assigned to specific individuals. These individuals are responsible for contacting their respective people to verify that they are alive and to determine their condition, if they are injured. These group leaders use smart devices to text and call people on their lists. The call tree can also be loaded in the app, and the app stores the counts as the group leaders provide them.

4.7 Mobile Healthcare

The healthcare industry is rapidly implementing and integrating smart devices into their environments. Healthcare sees smart devices, first and foremost, as an easy way for healthcare practitioners to record information when it happens without violating any compliance requirements. Smart devices are being used in patient treatment, patient monitoring, patient record management, patient appointment management, surveillance, etc. Five days, two days, and a day before an appointment with the doctor, a text message can be sent reminding the patient of the appointment and requesting a confirmation. About 52% of healthcare practitioners responding to the Healthcare Information and Management Systems Society (HIMSS) survey in December 2012 said that smart devices made "substantial impact," and another 16% said that smart devices had a "dramatic impact" on patient care.

The healthcare industry has realized the many benefits of using smart devices and connecting to patients through smart devices. Because of the many regulatory requirements, healthcare providers and professionals must implement smart devices in a very secure manner so as to prevent loss, tampering, and unauthorized access to patients' medical information and patients' personal identifiable information. In spite of the many compliance requirements, health-care providers and professionals see many benefits to implementing a secure infrastructure for smart devices.

Also, in the healthcare environment, smart devices provide the benefits of the ease of use and bringing the information at our finger-tips. Before a medical professional sees a patient, the practitioner can pull up the patient's medical record on a tablet and view the medical history, as well as the personal history, as the practitioner is walking over to see the patient. They can update the patient record as they are talking to the patient. Tablets are lighter and smaller than a lap-top and, as such, are convenient. This was one of the reasons that we were approached by hospitals to assist them in creating a smart device infrastructure that supports their various locations. We will discuss secure mobile device infrastructure in the coming chapters, but suffice it to say that convenience for the medical practitioner was one of the reasons for the project and a requirement in the design.

Smart devices help healthcare practitioners provide individual, as well as group, communication. It assists healthcare providers in creating and maintaining an escalation chain so that the right people are contacted in an emergency or when needed. Healthcare providers also use smart devices to efficiently filter alerts so that only the real issues are escalated. In fact, even when the doctor is not in the hospital, a snapshot of the patient information, graph, moni-tor, etc., can be sent to the doctor for evaluation. Because current smart devices have very clear pictures, the doctor can quickly form an opinion.

Smart devices also help healthcare providers manage their own resources efficiently. Providers must address the challenges related to the coordination of resources. A provider has to coordinate everything from the registrar to pathology, from visiting specialists to registered nurses, etc. Smart devices are used to quickly identify and resolve schedules and any issues that could affect patient care. Smart devices provide a means for the provider and the practitioner to take notes.

Smart devices also have another impact on individuals' health in the form of wearables. Wearables are a form of smart devices that we can wear like a watch or a headband. These wearables, while providing the standard time information, perform other functions such as monitoring heart rate, reading blood pressure, and counting the number of steps that a person has taken in a day and at what speed. We know the public wearables such as Fitbit, Apple Watch, Samsung Watch, and Garmin. However, there are also many wearables in the healthcare industry for specific purposes. One of these lesser known devices is the Leaf Healthcare Ulcer Sensor (Figure 4.9).

This wearable is designed to inform the wearer when it is time to move around. Embrace is another wearable that is geared toward healthcare. Embrace is a watch-type wearable with strong sensors. The technology includes Bluetooth, as well as a gyroscope, and provides the ability for an authorized third party to monitor the readings. For example, a parent with an epileptic child can monitor the readings and know when the child is about to have a seizure.

The trend is for wearables (Figure 4.10) to send information directly to the healthcare provider. An example is QuardioCore, which is a wearable that is strapped on your chest and monitors your heart health. It is an electrocardiogram with information in the cloud so that the doctor can monitor the patient. Smart devices are increasing the information available to the doctor so that the doctor can make informed decisions. Because the healthcare industry is always changing, with new drugs and new instructions, the medical practitioner must be knowledgeable. Smart devices aggregate all the new

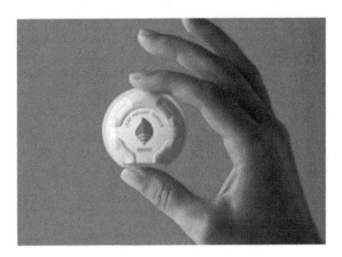

Figure 4.9   Leaf Healthcare Ulcer Sensor.

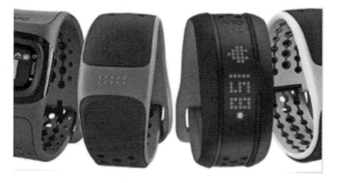

Figure 4.10 Examples of wearable smart devices.

information into one small, easy-to-use platform and at the palm of the practitioner's hands.

4.8 Location Information

Location! Location! Location! Anybody that has any association with the real-estate industry, either as a buyer or a seller, is familiar with that phrase. But, smart devices, through the integration of the Global Positioning System (GPS) software, provide the ability to identify the location of the device (Figure 4.11). For the safety of their children, some parents may use tracking apps available for smart devices. This

Figure 4.11 Smart devices can be located through use of cell towers and GPS software.

allows the parent some peace of mind knowing that the parent can identify the location of the child for safety reasons.

Smart devices provide monitoring in different forms. With the introduction of the Internet of things and every home and home appliance connected to the Internet, smart devices provide a means to monitor from anywhere. With sensors and cameras installed in your home, the collected data and video are displayed on your smart device in real time. If there is a break-in to your home, an alert is sent to your smart device, as well as the authorities, and the video of the events is immediately streamed to your smart device. Users are starting to use smart devices to monitor the house in case of a burst water pipe or to make sure that their pet is doing okay in the house. Some of the home devices that can be connected to your smart device include Nest Thermostats and Nest Protect. Cable and cell service providers are now providing *intelligent* home monitoring that includes the ability to lock and unlock doors from your smart device (Figure 4.12). According to some of these security monitoring companies, going

Figure 4.12   Monitoring homes using smart devices.

wireless with home security is better than connecting to landlines because there is no line for the intruder to cut.

Law enforcement is finding smart devices to be very helpful. Imagine that you are a police detective on an investigation. The criminal's cell phone contains a lot of information that can help the officer solve the case quickly. The smartphone will provide information on the path that the criminal traveled by showing a log of all the cell towers used by the smartphone and at what time. The smart device also logs all the calls and texts that are received by the individual, which will provide a tremendous amount of information to the detective.

Location information is now married to social media, and, as such, some location apps also have social media built in. A good example of the merging of location information in smart devices and social media is Waze, a navigation application that not only provides you turn-by-turn information to your destination but also has social media aspects. Users of Waze can identify a location where a police officer may be waiting for traffic violators and warn incoming vehicles. This shows up on the display screen of every person running the Waze app on their smart device. It also warns the driver before they approach the spot where the police officer may be. In addition, the users of the app (also called Wazers) can provide other information to other motorists such as the location of accidents, traffic jam, hazards on the road, vehicles parked on the shoulder, and road closure. In addition, Waze allows the user to create his or her social group. When a member of the social group is on the road and with their Waze app running, you are immediately notified. This extends the use of geolocation information.

Smart devices obtain geolocation information from various sources. In essence, anybody with the right app can track a smart device and, as such, the owner of the smart device. The sources of location information for a smart device include the following:

- *GPS:* This source uses satellites to provide location information.
- *Assisted and synthetic GPS:* These are tools that help improve the time required to obtain GPS information. They predict where the next satellite location is days and weeks ahead. This reduces the connection and download times between the smart devices and the satellite.

- *Cell IDs:* Carriers assign cell IDs to smart devices, and they can use this information to determine the distance between any two smart devices. This also provides information as to the location of the cell ID or smart device.
- *Wi-fi:* Uses received signal strength indicators that the smartphone gets from nearby access points to search for the access point's location. It can also use wireless fingerprinting and the profile of defined places to provide location information.
- *Inertia sensors:* Smartphones have a built-in gyroscope, compass, and accelerometer to provide location information in places where wireless systems are unavailable.
- *Altimeter:* Provides height location information, especially if you are moving from one floor to another.

The location information is also used by smart device apps to let the tourist get directions and obtain the listings of nearby restaurants, gas stations, automated teller machines, and other related information.

Smart devices, as we have seen, have become an integral part of modern-day society and provide a lot of benefits for the user. The ease of use for smart devices has made them the tool for modern society, and smart devices will continue to evolve both as a business tool and a personal entertainment device. As they are miniaturized, their importance and usage for medical diagnostics and as an early warning device will also increase. Smart devices will continue to provide us information quickly and easily.

5

RISKS ASSOCIATED WITH THE USE OF SMART DEVICES

5.1 Introduction

Imagine that you are the security officer at your company, and you have worked hard to build a *Fort Knox* around the perimeter of your network. Excellent! You are feeling good. Then, the organization wants to allow remote access to the users who want to work from home or remote locations. You design the appropriate solution without compromising your network security.

But then, the top management and the sales department want you to allow access for smart devices to connect to your network and read emails or download data from your network. You sweat a little but eventually implement a mobile device management (MDM) solution to address the access for smartphones and tablets. You defined and developed profiles for each group of users and defined the type of access that is granted to the group through their mobile devices. Some users can only read emails, whereas others have additional network access to your company's information.

And then, the wearables come out, and nobody says anything to you, but your users are buying and connecting their wearables to their smartphones. What can possibly go wrong?

But, before we go into detail about the different risks associated with smart devices, let us talk about risk. How do we define risk? *Merriam-Webster Dictionary* defines risk as "the possibility that something bad or unpleasant (such as an injury or a loss) will happen; someone or something that may cause something bad or unpleasant to happen; a person or thing that someone judges to be a good or bad choice for insurance, a loan, etc."* Risk is a situation that exposes a person, a company, or something to danger, harm, or loss.

---

* http://www.merriam-webster.com/dictionary/risk

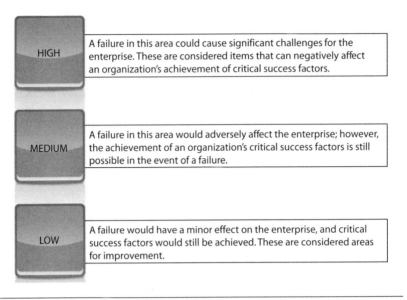

HIGH

A failure in this area could cause significant challenges for the enterprise. These are considered items that can negatively affect an organization's achievement of critical success factors.

MEDIUM

A failure in this area would adversely affect the enterprise; however, the achievement of an organization's critical success factors is still possible in the event of a failure.

LOW

A failure would have a minor effect on the enterprise, and critical success factors would still be achieved. These are considered areas for improvement.

Figure 5.1 Risk categories with a detailed description.

For information security, risk is the product of the likelihood and the impact of a threat against corporate information technology (IT) assets. The likelihood of a threat increases as the exploitable vulnerabilities for the threat increase. Say, for example, when you perform a vulnerability scan, and the scan output shows many Secure Sockets Layer (SSL) vulnerabilities, this means that there is an increased risk that IT infrastructure can be exploited using an SSL exploit. Depending on the type of threat and the number of vulnerabilities, a risk can be classified as high, medium, or low depending on the organization's nomenclature, as shown in Figure 5.1.

Smart devices pose a lot of security risks to organizations and individuals. Wearable devices are not especially designed with information security in mind. These devices are designed with the ease of use in mind and nothing else. As such, the operating systems for smart devices can be hacked, and the traffic to and from the device can be monitored and intercepted. The risks associated with smart devices include the following:

- Expansion of the threat surface
- Data loss due to device loss
- Unintentional disclosure of data
- Improper disposal and decommissioning of device

- Phishing attacks
- Spoofing attacks
- Malware attacks
- Spyware attacks
- Network attacks
- Encryption and sensitive data protection
- Litigation and retention
- Lack of user awareness

5.2 Expansion of the Threat Surface

It's alive! It's alive! It's alive! Yes, smart devices are alive and talking. Not only are they alive and talking, but others are also listening. Who is listening? Friend or foe, we may not know. Smart devices increase the number of vulnerabilities that can affect an organization, as well as expand and extend the attack surface (Figure 5.2). Smart devices, including wearables, have built-in communication systems that include Bluetooth, near-field communication (NFC), and Wi-fi. Remember our story at the beginning of this chapter about employees connecting their wearables to their smartphones that have been granted access to corporate data? Now, imagine a very intelligent attacker (most of them are) realizing that the weakest link in your organization's network connectivity is the wearable devices. The attacker then launches various attacks on the wearables and gains access to them. The attacker has gained access not only to the wearables but also to the smartphone that is connected to the wearable. By the same token, when the user connects to the corporate network, the attacker also gains access to the corporate network. So much for our Fort Knox. In essence, every smart device that directly or indirectly connects to the network is

Risk progression path

Figure 5.2 The regression path of smart devices into a corporate network.

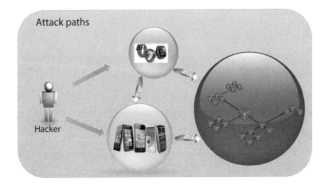

Figure 5.3   The regression path of compromised smart devices into a corporate network.

another point from which to be attacked. Smart devices increase the available attack paths for the hacker (Figure 5.3).

Let us look at other scenarios. When you walk into your closest hardware store or talk to your favorite home monitoring company, you will notice that the new thing is the connected door locks that use your home Wi-fi. Yes, it allows you the ease to lock and unlock your front door from your smartphone. However, this connected smart device (lock) is also connected to your home Wi-fi, which is used to connect to the company network. For each smart thing we connect to the network, we expand the attack surface for a would-be intruder. These devices are usually sold with default configurations, and the buyer/user may not know about the security implications of these devices. The fact that many of these devices are made in China should send shudders down corporate spines. But that is a topic for another time. Remember that weakest link? Here it is again.

5.3 Data Loss due to Device Loss

In 2014, *Consumer Reports* reported that about 3.1 million Americans lost their smart devices due to theft in 2013. Of this number, *Consumer Reports* estimates that about 1.4 million devices were never recovered. At present, most families and organizations have been affected by a smart device theft. Smartphones, for example, contain everything that most people need for their daily information. They have emails, contacts, social media connections, credit cards as in Apple Pay and

Samsung Pay, etc. The smart device is our Rolodex, email, news media, music store, sales guru, and information robot, all wrapped into one device. We have become very dependent on smart devices. They are like an appendage that is our current addiction. There is so much information about us, our lives, friends, family, and our work that is stored in the smart device, and hackers know that also.

Now, imagine our earlier scenarios in a connected world. Your wearable is connected to your smartphone, which is connected to the corporate network. You have the ability to download data from the corporate network and access to the corporate directory. Your responsibilities in the company as the head of sales and marketing give access to information that, under normal circumstances, should not be disclosed to most people within your company and, let alone, outsiders like your competitors. Then, the unthinkable happens. You lose your smart device because it was stolen. You are now one of the statistics that will never get their smart device back. Assuming that the smart device falls into unscrupulous hands, not only are your personal information and social network life exposed but also your company. The theft can result in providing the hacker information on how to breach your corporate network and data. Once in, the hacker will hide in the corporate network so that he or she will not be found. The intruder will then go after the information that they want and send it to themselves. Monitoring your network activities, especially for activities going out of your network, is an eye-opener for a lot of organizations. Such traffic monitoring will identify what information is leaking from your organization. Your security is as good as your weakest link. The lost smart devices now become the weakest link.

Let us assume that you are a homeowner who has installed smart locks for the outside doors to your house. The smart locks are connected to your smartphone, which you use to lock and unlock the doors. It allows you to unlock the door for somebody (e.g., cleaning lady) who does not have a key to your house, and you do not need to be there to unlock the door. What happens if the smartphone is stolen? The thief now has access to your house and can even change the password and lock you out of your own house. Smart devices are becoming an intruder's gold mine.

5.4 Unintentional Disclosure of Data

We all have seen somebody rubbernecking on the plane or at some crowded public place. When flying on a plane, and you start using your smart device to respond to emails or text messages, somebody close to you starts getting interested in your communication. If this is company-confidential communication, you definitely do not want the rubbernecker to see the communication. In other scenarios, you leave your smart device out and walk away. You do not have any screen lock set. Somebody else comes over and browses the information on your smart device and sees the confidential information. Let us assume that a text message came in informing you that your attention is needed for some company deal. The intruder can then see that confidential deal and can use this information to their own advantage. Maybe your company is buying another company, and now the intruder can go purchase the stocks of the company being purchased. The intruder has inside information because the information was disclosed unintentionally.

5.5 Improper Disposal and Decommissioning of Device

These days, smart devices are obsolete in six months, and individuals and organizations are perpetually upgrading and replacing their devices. We replace because our previous one was lost, or does not support the new features, or we just want the new, shiny one. What happens to the decommissioned smart devices? How do organizations account for them? If this is a personal device with access to company data, how does the organization safeguard its information when the user replaces their old device?

Most individuals and companies do not properly dispose of smart devices. Some organizations do not have asset disposal policy and procedures, and those that don't include smart devices as a part of the organization's assets.

Data are an asset that the organization should protect. When an organization's data touch a smart device or any other IT asset, there should be a procedure that addresses how to remove sensitive information, if not all company information, from the smart device before disposal or storage. Many organizations and individuals buy used smart devices, and, if the smart device is not properly formatted, company and personal information may fall into the hands of a would-be intruder. Imagine that you sold your old device that has connectivity to your company on eBay but did not wipe or reset the smart device; now, the buyer has a smart device that grants them access to your personal and corporate information. A decommissioned smart device can be the weakest link to your information security.

5.6 Phishing Attacks

Phishing is fraudulent misrepresentations through emails or short message service (SMS) messages by attackers in order to deceive and obtain information such as user login credentials, account, and personal information. This is usually achieved by masquerading as a legitimate user. The unaware recipient of such an email or SMS message will respond with the assumption that he or she is responding to a valid and known user. Attackers use phishing attacks to gain access to corporate networks because they know that most organizations now spend money to protect their perimeter while the internal network may be unprotected, and, by gaining valid credentials to the internal network, they now have access from within the organization. The attacker will install their own application within many computers in the organization so that they can gain direct access without using the phishing attack anymore. The attacker may continue the attack until an administrator's credential is obtained. Once the attacker obtains the administrator credential, he or she creates multiple administrator accounts in many systems that will be used to collect company data, monitor emails, and even ransom the organization's data. When the attacker ransoms the data, a payment must be made before access to the data is returned.

Phishing attacks are not only used to gain access to the organization's network but may also be utilized to obtain money by deceiving the recipient of the phishing message. Imagine that you have a PayPal account, and you receive a message that is shown in Figure 5.4. Of course, you will panic, and, if in that panic, you click on the button that says "Log In to PayPal" (Figure 5.5), the attacker now has your PayPal account and password. In no time, the attacker will drain all the accounts that are connected to your PayPal account.

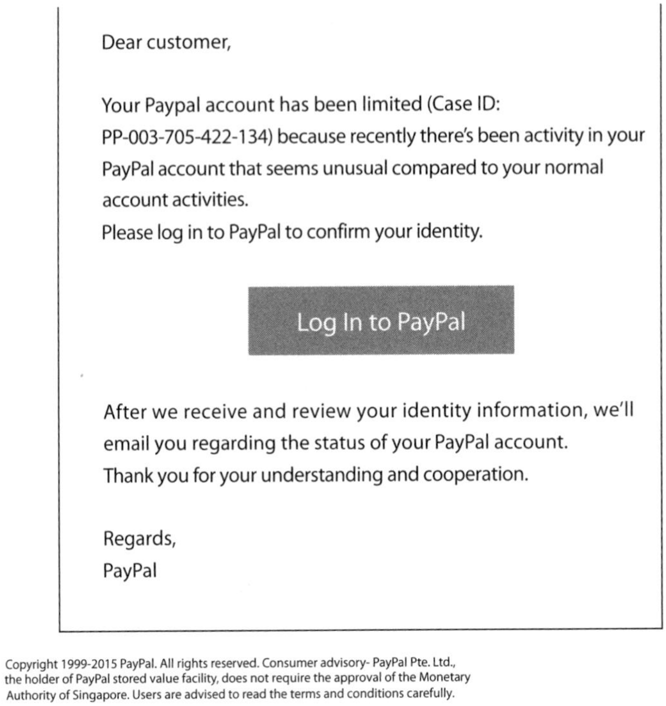

Dear customer,

Your Paypal account has been limited (Case ID: PP-003-705-422-134) because recently there's been activity in your PayPal account that seems unusual compared to your normal account activities.
Please log in to PayPal to confirm your identity.

Log In to PayPal

After we receive and review your identity information, we'll email you regarding the status of your PayPal account.
Thank you for your understanding and cooperation.

Regards,
PayPal

Copyright 1999-2015 PayPal. All rights reserved. Consumer advisory- PayPal Pte. Ltd., the holder of PayPal stored value facility, does not require the approval of the Monetary Authority of Singapore. Users are advised to read the terms and conditions carefully.

Figure 5.4 PayPal phishing attack.

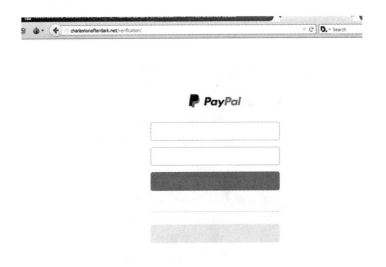

Figure 5.5 Fake PayPal logon screen.

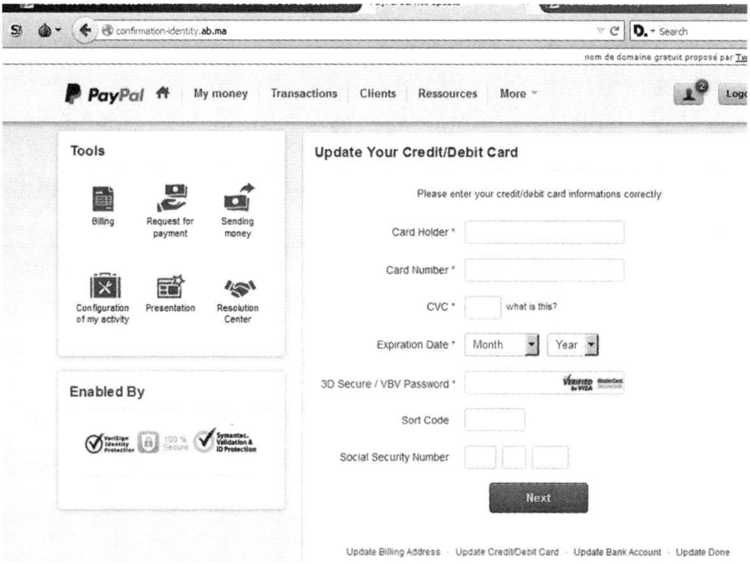

Figure 5.6   Fake PayPal information update screen.

5.7 Spoofing Attacks

This attack method is when the attacker pretends to be somebody whom he or she is not. Wikipedia defines spoofing attack as a "situation in which one person or program successfully masquerades as another by falsifying data, thereby gaining a legitimate advantage."* Imagine that you are the chief executive officer (CEO) of a large corporation, and you are overseas on business. An attacker sends a phishing message to your administrator asking her to wire $4 million to an account in overseas that you need to complete the deal. The message looks like it is coming from you, the CEO. If the CEO's administrator wires the money, then the money goes to the attackers. Spoofing attacks may be combined with other attacks. For example, a phishing attack can be combined with a spoofing attack. Our PayPal example was actually spoofing PayPal (Figure 5.6). A caller ID or an email can be spoofed. It requires the attacker to perform a little due diligence on the Internet and the company Website, and much of the information needed can be obtained. The caller ID may require a little more digging.

---

* https://en.wikipedia.org/wiki/Spoofing_attack

5.8 Malware Attacks

A survey published by *Consumer Reports* in 2014 found that 34% of smartphone owners have no malware protection. Kaspersky puts this number at 40%. These users do not have a firewall or antivirus program installed. Take a look at iTunes and Google Play Store, and you will find many malware protection programs. These include Avast, Kaspersky, Trent Micro, Norton, and many others. These users do not know of or do not care about exposing their smart devices to malware. The same *Consumer Reports* survey found that only about 36% have set a four-digit PIN that locks their phone. The risk is extremely high for the people who have not installed a malware program and set a passcode.

Imagine that these unprotected smart devices are also used to connect to the corporate network. Then, the attacker can infect the corporate network with a malware with a virus and force the whole organization to devote resources to finding the source of the virus and eradicate it. Of course, the source is a smart device. This may be possible because not only is the smart device not protected with an antivirus and firewall program, but the organization may also not check for viruses from smart devices. This will definitely be a bad idea.

The malware attack may be for financial reasons. Some smart devices have personal information, as well as credit card information, PIN numbers, and bank accounts in the smart device. Add to that the introduction of Apple Pay and Samsung Pay. While Apple Pay and Samsung Pay may have encrypted information, the attacker can still copy the encrypted information and try to decrypt it on his or her own time. The malware may also be one that makes charges from your smart device using the credit card information obtained from your smart device. A small business suffered this attack. The charges made to this illegitimate charity organization were $1.00 and $1.50 so as not to raise any suspicion. The total amount was over $5,000, and this was within a two-week period. The idea is to fly under the radar so that nobody will notice.

5.9 Spyware Attacks

Spyware allows an intruder to covertly obtain information from a user's computer. Spyware generally does not spread like a virus.

In some cases, spyware may be targeted against a user, a computer, or a company, but, in general, spyware is used for unwanted advertisements, collecting personal information, or modifying the computer. Spyware will generally phone home once the target is acquired and information has been obtained. Some spyware will make changes to the target computer and is generally difficult to remove. Spyware can be acquired through a phishing attack. Once the user clicks on the link in the phishing attack, the spyware is installed. Imagine that you found a music video that you want online, and you click to play or download the music video. However, in playing that music video, you also installed spyware in the background.

Initially, smart device operating systems were attacked with spyware. Apple controlled such influx because of how apps are approved before the app is introduced in iTunes. Google's Android operating system, on the other hand, is an open system that allowed anybody to develop what they want. This was taken advantage of by spyware developers. Spyware that will monitor your smart device usage, keystroke, copy contact information, or financial information was created. I fail to understand why an Android game requires access to my contact list, but you will find situations like that when installing an Android app. If the smart device is connected to a corporate network, the spyware will collect all the necessary information that a hacker will need to break into a corporate network. The weakest link could be what users download and install on their smart devices.

When a single individual or corporation is targeted, the spyware attack becomes a surveillance attack. The surveillance attack may or may not be for criminal intentions. Law enforcement can use surveillance to obtain information about criminals for prosecution. Competitors can use surveillance to target certain individuals within competing companies. Surveillance may not be directly aimed at the target party but rather the third-party vendor that supplies goods and services. At present, attackers look for any and all avenues that can provide access to the target an individual or corporation. Surveillance attacks can be used to log keystrokes, record voice conversations, log and copy SMS messages, copy files, track location, and log and observe activities on the Internet.

Search the app section of Apple's iTunes, Google's Play Store, or Windows Store, and you will find thousands of apps. For apps to be listed for iTunes and Windows, the application has to be certified. This does not mean that these controls cannot be bypassed. Google does not have such corporate reviews, but users review these apps, and Google publishes those reviews. Some of these applications may not be what they say they are. These apps can be Trojan horses that carry bad and malicious processes. What you see is not what you are getting. These rogue applications can be used to introduce advance persistent threats (APTs), and nobody will know or suspect. The APT will then send information to its home base, and nobody is the wiser. Companies have lost their crown jewels to competitors or China because an APT was somehow introduced to their environment.

Here is another scenario. For those who travel a lot, and who are constantly on the plane and in hotel rooms, you will have noticed that the hotels give you free Internet, and there is Internet that you can purchase on the plane. These make our work lives easier, and we appreciate all that, but have you ever asked how secure these networks are? If I connect my smart device or laptop to these semipublic networks, can somebody else be snooping around trying to capture traffic, credit card information, or your login credentials to your company's network? If a hacker is connected to the same network, the hacker could be collecting Internet protocol (IP) packets that he or she can then analyze later. Imagine being in the plane with all these business people traveling on Monday to their clients and coming back Thursday or Friday, or going to one of the busy hotels between Monday and Thursday to collect information from other hotel guests without their permission. There are hacking tools that will display all Wi-fi traffic, as well as the IP addresses of connected hosts. The hacker can also probe other guests' smart devices and computers to see which are open, and, when the hacker finds one, installs an APT, captures credentials for later use, or whatever the hacker intends to do. It is not a pretty picture, but it is important to identify any and all weak links.

5.10 Network Attacks

Yet another risk associated with smart devices is network attacks. All the previous risks discussed in this chapter have a network implication because each is using the network to find and steal information.

This can create additional traffic and bandwidth usage that can slow the network down. An attacker can launch a denial-of-service attack on a network by attacking the smart devices that are connected to the network.

Smart devices come with Bluetooth and Wi-fi, which provide the ease of connectivity and use for the smart device. These same networking tools create risks for the smart device and any network in the back end. Bluetooth, while providing convenient access to the device, can also be used by an attack to break into the device. The Bluetooth, when on, is discoverable. An attacker will try various available means to break into the device through the Bluetooth.

In addition, smart devices are equipped with Wi-fi networking capabilities. Most homes, as well as most organizations, have one, if not multiple, Wi-fi networks. The Wi-fi networks at individuals' homes and most organizations are private. On the other hand, some retail businesses, airports, and cities provide public Wi-fi networks. While private networks have more security, most public Wi-fi networks do not have any security. An attacker can go to a Starbucks coffee shop and monitor the traffic of everybody who uses the free network. If your employee decides to use the public Wi-fi, the attack can capture your login traffic, as well as any information that the attacker deems important. This will include credit card information, personal data, etc. While Wi-fi hotspots provide convenient connection to the Internet and back-end network, they also pose considerable risks.

Home Wi-fi networks may not be properly secured. Many home Wi-fi networks are still implemented with Wired Equivalent Privacy (WEP) encryption. Even the access points (APs) implemented with Wi-fi Protected Access (WPA) and Wi-fi Protected Access 2 (WPA2) may not have strong passphrases. As such, an attacker can try different passphrases in other to gain access. Imagine that your outside doors are equipped with connected doors, and an attacker hacks your network; the attack can now access your locks. Future burglars will not need a crowbar but instead a laptop or other smart devices and hacking tools to unlock your door. The attacker may even change the password to the lock and lock you out of your own house.

Another scenario will be Wi-fi-connected cars and self-driving cars. The wave of the future is cars with their own Wi-fi APs and cars that drive themselves. Imagine that an attacker hacks into the car and takes over the car. The risk exists that such an attack could create accidents on the road and may result in loss of life.

The following are some of the network attacks that may be initiated from or involve a smart device:

- *Denial of service (DoS):* The attempt to make a computer system or network services unavailable to the intended and appropriate users. This attack can be in the form of the computing system being intentionally flooded with more request than it can immediately address. As a result, the computer system slows to a crawl.
- *Man in the middle:* As the name implies, the attack goes between the source and destination of a computer communication. The attacker secretly relays the message from the source to the destination and sometimes modifies the communication between the source and the destination. As Figure 5.7 shows, the intended path for the traffic (light gray line) is supposed to go straight from the *source* to the *destination*, but the attacker intercepts and relays (dark gray lines) the communication packets after possibly modifying them.
- *Network sniffing:* This is accomplished by using packet sniffing tools to capture and view network data at the packet

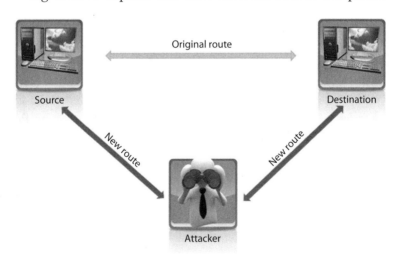

Figure 5.7 Visual representation of a man-in-the-middle attack.

level. These tools are designed to be legitimately used for network diagnostics, but attackers use them to capture packets for a network and a host IP that the attacker is interested in. In our hotel example, discussed earlier in this section, the attacker will set his or her network card in a promiscuous mode and then capture the network packets of all or some of the hotel guests.

- *Bluesnarfing:* When an intruder steals information from a smart device through a Bluetooth connection, it is called bluesnarfing. Bluetooth provides a high-speed connection, but the range is very short. The smart devices where the Bluetooth protocol is always on are susceptible to bluesnarfing. An attacker can gain access to the calendar, contact list, email, SMS messages, etc., by exploiting a smart device through bluesnarfing.

- *Bluejacking:* Bluejacking is a way to send unsolicited messages to a Bluetooth-enabled device without pairing with the target smart device. This can be used to send unsolicited messages and spam the target device. Bluejacking is another way of delivering malware to a smart device.

- *Bluebugging:* By default, Bluetooth is enabled in discovery mode on smart devices. Bluebugging provides the ability for a hacker to send commands to the smart device that can remotely control a smart device, send and read text messages, place phone calls, and monitor phone calls. Remember the example that we gave about the CEO whose account was spoofed, and his administrator was asked to wire money to the CEO? Bluebugging makes the situation worse because the messages will be coming from the CEO's smart device, and so the administrator will assume that it was an authentic request. Worse still, bluebugging does not leave any trace of the hacker.

- *WEP/WPA attack:* WEP and WPA are two of the available Wi-fi security protocols. Many vulnerabilities have been identified for these protocols. WEP is vulnerable to passive attacks to decrypt traffic, active attacks to decrypt traffic, active attacks to inject traffic, and dictionary-based attacks.

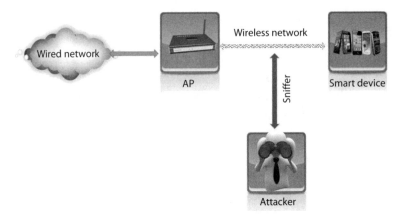

Figure 5.8   Visual representation of a Wi-fi attack.

WPA is vulnerable to brute-force attacks to obtain the shared secret or passphrase. Figure 5.8 shows a Wi-fi attack.

- *Near-field communication:* The NFC, as was discussed in Chapter 4, is used by many devices and companies for credit and debit card purchases (e.g., Apple Pay, Samsung Pay). NFC works in card emulation mode, reader/writer mode, and peer-to-peer mode. Hackers can use relay attacks and brute-force attacks on NFC-enabled smart devices. The end result is that the attacker steals money using NFC.

- *Rogue access point:* Unauthorized APs are created in two ways. First, an attacker can create an SSID for a known business Wi-fi, and, when visitors who connect to this rogue AP enter their passwords or credit card information, the attacker captures this information for later use. The attacker can also try to break into the device and install malware to grant the attacker access in the future. The second way rogue APs are used is within the organization. If an organization does not monitor its network ports and available Wi-fi networks, an intruder or an employee can plug in an AP to one of the network ports and set up a Wi-fi that connects to the organization network infrastructure and can grant access to outsiders. The organization does not have any control of the rogue APs or the configuration.

5.11 Encryption and Sensitive Data Protection

What constitutes sensitive data may differ between one organization and another, and between one industry and another. For the health-care industry, the Health Insurance Portability and Accountability Act and personal health information are important, while, for the financial industry, personally identifiable information and financial information are important. The protection of this sensitive information is not guaranteed because the user-owned device may not have any type of encryption for data that are stored on the device or data that are in motion between the device and the corporate network. As such, the information can be intercepted and viewed by an unauthorized user. While it is possible to use digital certificates on smart devices, most smart device owners do not implement certificate-based encryption or authentication. Without encryption, sensitive data are exposed on smart devices because, by default, the manufacturer smart device installation instructions are geared toward the ease of installation and use, and not for security. Lack of encryption will allow an attack to passively monitor and capture sensitive data and credentials.

5.12 Litigation and Retention

What happens if a smart device is used in stealing company intellectual property? What if the smart device is a personal device that has been granted access to a corporate network? Can the corporation seize the user's personal smart device? What legal rights does the user have and what legal recourse does the corporation have? Depending on the situation, the organization may not have any legal recourse, especially if the organization does not have a well-written smart device usage policy. Take a situation where a document of importance has passed the retention period, and the organization has asked everybody to delete the document. What if this document has already been copied by an employee to a smart device, and the employee refuses to delete such documents? What legal recourse does the organization have against the employee? What if the employee releases such confidential information to the public that results in the organization making the evening news? This is a risk that many organizations face when personal smart devices are allowed to connect to corporate networks and download or view data.

One of the issues with the implementation of smart devices is a lack of documented security standards. Organizations do not define the standard devices and smart device operating systems that will be allowed. Organizations also do not create a minimum security baseline for each device type and version that will govern how the device is secured. What about allowed software? Most organizations do not define a *whitelist* or *blacklist* of allowed apps. The result is that users install whatever apps strike their fancy without knowing the impact of such app on corporate information security. Some MDM solutions have the ability to containerize the apps on the device between personal and corporate apps, with a *Chinese wall* between the two areas. But, without such demarcations between personal use and corporate use, the work of the legal department is made even harder. Data and apps for both personal and organizational use are intermingled without a clear definition of ownership. It begs the question, "Who owns what on the smart device?"

5.13 Lack of User Awareness

User awareness is important in securing smart devices. Generally, manufacturers do not provide adequate information to users about all the security features available on the device and all other security software that the user may need to purchase. Device manufacturers do not include the consequences of not properly securing a smart device. These manufacturers do not educate device users about access control, firewall, antivirus, patching, and device authentication.

Some organizations also implement smart devices as company owned, or BYOD, but fail to educate the user about the security requirements of using the devices. The organizations do not answer the questions about "What will smart devices do for us?" and "How are we going to implement and secure these devices?" The implementing and securing should include security awareness training for users. Most organizations do not know what security features are built in the smart devices and, a lot of times, rush the implementation because a powerful executive or powerful business group wants it.

Now, we know that many smart devices, like any other technology, pose a lot of risks to both the individual and an organization. Each of the risks is a result of somebody not paying attention to the security implications of smart devices to the organization or the individual. In each case, the risk can result in the loss of personal data, the loss of intellectual property or sensitive and classified information, the loss of financial information and assets, and a loss of reputation.

PART II

SECURITY OF SMART DEVICES

Before the rise of smart devices, threats to mobile phones were relatively small, when compared to computers, as the devices could not be programmed by anyone other than the manufacturer, and the phone networks were controlled by the carrier. At present, smart devices are not only very similar to personal computers and offer many of the same functionalities, but both also have much of the same risk of being attacked by similar threat vectors. Malware can affect a smart device via Short Message Service messages, Multimedia Messaging Service messages, email, and even Web pages.

The convenience of portable smart devices with a large number of functionalities assists users in performing day-to-day functions such as emails, social networking, and banking. Because of this, users input and store sensitive information on their smart devices. A large number of users prefer to use their smart device to access nearly all services, thus making it a desirable target for attackers.

Smartphones collect and compile a vast amount of sensitive information. As the amount of information grows, so does the need to protect the vast amount of sensitive information that reside on these devices. Current-generation smart devices combine software, hardware, and network services to ensure the maximum security.

Chapter 6 will concentrate on the various hardware security features available in various popular platforms. Chapter 7 will cover the software and network features. Chapter 8 will discuss how to secure smart devices.

6

HARDWARE FEATURES

6.1 Introduction

To understand hardware features, it is necessary to first understand the boot process of a smart device.

6.2 Secure Boot Process

The process of starting a smart device and putting it into a state of readiness for operation is known as the boot process. Also important in this process is the system partition, which is the partitioning of the disk volume containing hardware-specific files that are needed to boot the operating system. A verified boot ensures the integrity of the smart device software starting from a hardware root of trust up to the system partition. Malware with root privileges can avoid detection programs and otherwise mask themselves. The malware can accomplish this because it is often more privileged than the detectors, allowing the software to misrepresent itself to detection programs. During a secure booting process, each phase confirms the integrity of the next phase before executing it. Android calls this feature a *verified boot*, while Apple's iOS refers to their fairly similar feature as the *secure boot chain*. This process helps safeguard that the lowest levels of software have not been altered or compromised by malware. Apple iOS and Android take different approaches to responding to errors that are found during the secure boot process.

For Apple iOS, if any step of this boot process is unable to load or verify the next process, startup is immediately halted, and the device displays the *Connect to iTunes* screen. When this occurs, the device has entered recovery mode or a device firmware upgrade depending on

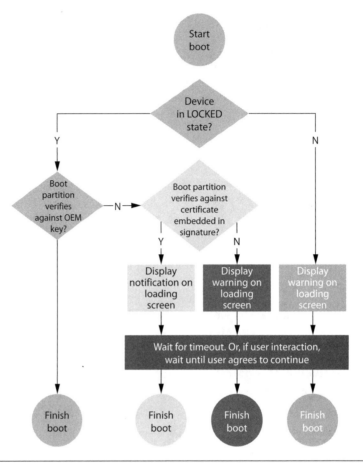

Figure 6.1 Android verified boot flowchart provided by Google.

what portion of the processes failed. Once this error message appears, you are forced to recover the device to resume operation.

In the Android environment, if verification fails at any phase, the user will be visibly notified and always be given the choice to continue using the device at their own discretion. The logic diagram (Figure 6.1) shows the Android boot process.

6.3 Cryptography

Smart devices are getting faster and more powerful every day, and, as the strength of the hardware improves, so does the device's ability to secure itself. The backbone of cryptography for smart devices is its hardware. Strong hardware is needed to complete the cryptographic processes, which are extremely complicated and labor intensive. Let us take a look at the two similar operating systems (Apple and Android) and describe how each approaches the cryptography topic.

6.3.1 *Apple iOS*

According to Apple, "Every iOS device has a dedicated Advanced Encryption Standard (AES) 256 crypto engine built into the Direct Memory Access (DMA) path between the flash storage and main system memory. The device's unique ID (UID) and a device group ID (GID) are AES 256-bit keys fused (UID) or compiled (GID) into the application processor and Secure Enclave during manufacturing." Apple says, "No software or firmware can read them directly; they can see only the results of encryption or decryption operations performed by dedicated AES engines implemented in silicon using the UID or GID as a key. Additionally, the Secure Enclave's UID and GID can only be used by the AES engine dedicated to the Secure Enclave. The UIDs are unique to each device and are not recorded by Apple or any of its suppliers."*

The UID is very important to this process. The UID allows data to be cryptographically tied to a particular device. Apple makes sure that the key hierarchy protecting the file system includes the UID. This prevents someone from taking the memory chips and physically moving it from one device to another. If someone would attempt to move the chips, the files would be encrypted. The UID is not related to any other identifier on the device.

In combination with the stated hardware encryption built into iOS devices, Apple uses a technology that is referred to as *Data Protection* to protect the data stored on flash memory in iOS devices (Figure 6.2). Key preinstalled system apps (i.e., Mail, Calendar, Contacts, etc.) use Data Protection by default. Third-party apps installed on iOS 7 and later versions receive this protection automatically. Apple states, "Data Protection is implemented by constructing and managing a hierarchy of keys, and builds on the hardware encryption technologies built into each iOS device. Data Protection is controlled on a per-file basis by

---

* iOS Security, 2016. Available at https://www.apple.com/business/docs/iOS_Security
_Guide.pdf, retrieved July 1, 2016.

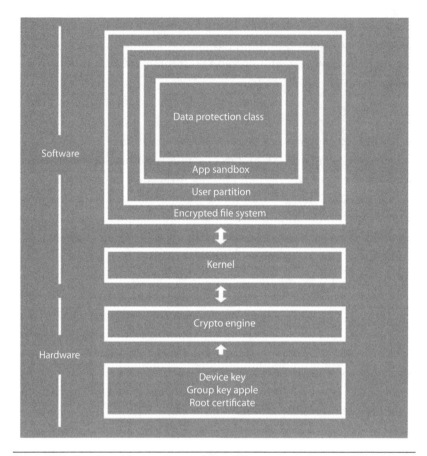

Figure 6.2 Security architecture diagram of Apple iOS.

assigning each file to a class; accessibility is determined by whether the class keys have been unlocked."

Unlike most of its competitors, all iOS devices are manufactured by Apple themselves. iOS devices are designed specifically to take advantage of the current and future mobile operating systems. This allows for a synergistic marriage between the operating system and hardware-based security that few others can match.

6.3.2 Android

The current versions of Android use full disk encryption; this is the process of encrypting all user data on an Android device using an encrypted key. Once the Android device is encrypted, all new user data are automatically encrypted before storing them to disk. When the data are accessed, they will automatically decrypt data.

Android states that "its full disk encryption is based on dm-crypt, which is a kernel feature that works at the block device layer."* This encryption works with embedded multimedia cards and other flash storage devices that present themselves to the kernel as block devices.

The encryption algorithm is 128 AES with cipher-block chaining and ESSIV: SHA256. The master key is encrypted with 128-bit AES via calls to the OpenSSL library. You must use 128 bits or more for the key (with 256 being optional).

On initial boot, the Android device creates a randomly generated 128-bit master key and then hashes it with a default password and stored salt. When the user creates the password or PIN on the device, only the 128-bit key is re-encrypted and stored.

6.4 Near-Field Communication

Near-field communication (NFC) is a technology that enables devices placed within a few centimeters of each other to exchange data (Figure 6.3). NFC offers convenience for connecting all types of consumer devices and enables rapid and easy communication. It is a standard-based short-range wireless connectivity technology. NFC evolved from radio-frequency identification, a technology that is used for the purposes of automatically identifying and tracking tags attached to objects in shipping companies, in large warehouses, and/or department stores to keep track of inventory. It uses electromagnetic induction in order to transmit information over a short space so that, by simply scanning a tag, a person can be provided with useful information such as the shipping container contents or the item identification number. NFC functions virtually the same way but is converted for the current-generation smartphones.

The standards for NFC are maintained by an organization called the NFC Forum. The members of this organization include some of the high-profile companies in the smartphone business including Apple, Google, Microsoft, and Samsung. NFC provides a normal

---

* Android: Full-Disk Encryption, available at https://source.android.com/security /encryption/full-disk.html.

NFC devices operate in 3 modes

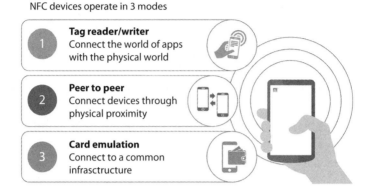

Figure 6.3 NFC operating mode diagram provided by the NFC Forum.

process for connecting consumer devices, via proximity, to link two devices. If your phone has an NFC chip, it could be used to transfer data to other phones or to NFC readers. In order for the connection to occur, both devices must be equipped with an NFC chip and be around a typical operating distance of 10 cm of each other. The maximum data exchange rate is approximately 424 kbit/s.

There are a great number of possibilities for the uses of NFC. This communication can either be one way or two way. For example, in a two-way NFC communication scenario, such as the simple transfer of contact information between two business associates, a person's smartphone would be set up to automatically exchange their personal business card information when an NFC connection is established. Once they encounter another person who also has their phone similarly configured, the users would only need to touch their phones together to exchange contact information. The recipients will then only have to accept the business card data and allow them to be entered into their phone book. In this scenario, both devices can read and write to each other.

In a one-way scenario, a person would store their credit card information on their smart device, and, once the connection is made to a credit card terminal, that information would be transmitted to the terminal to complete the purchase. This is perhaps the most popular use of NFC. NFC is the technology that makes the Apple Pay and Android Pay (discussed in Chapter 4) possible. The advantage that NFC has over similar technologies, such as Bluetooth and Wi-fi, is that NFC uses less power. This is important when you consider that phones are becoming more and more important for everyday tasks, and conserving battery life is essential.

NFC sounds great, but is it safe? Virtually any digital technology has the possibility to be hacked, and NFC is no exception. The close proximity needed to make an NFC connection is one of the strongest security features. For instance, a hacker would have to be extremely close to make the connection. NFC signals are extremely sensitive. If your device is pointed in the wrong direction, it is sometimes difficult to make the NFC connection. Other technologies can be accessed at a wider range such as Wi-fi or Bluetooth signals.

The proximity requirements are not enough to ensure the security of NFC. Every step in the process of an NFC transaction plays an important role. Hardware and software developers must use layers of password protection and encryption to their products and applications. Users should also be careful about who and what they make NFC connections with, as hackers could use this opportunity to attempt to steal a user's personal data. (See Chapter 5 for more on NFC.)

6.5 Authentication by Biometric Verification

Biometric authentication is a type of system that relies on the unique biological characteristics of individuals to verify identity for secure access to a smart device. Biometric authentication is convenient as there are no passwords to remember and theoretically should require that the designated person be present to authenticate the device. In a perfect world, all smart devices would use biometric authentication instead of passwords, but the accuracy and cost of readers make it difficult to implement. In the next section, we will go over some of the most popular uses of biometric authentication currently used in smart devices.

6.5.1 Apple Biometrics

Certain iOS devices have a technology called *Touch ID*; this is finger-print sensing (see Figure 6.4). This technology reads fingerprint data from any angle and is able to learn more about a person's fingerprint from each use. Touch ID works in conjunction with your system pass-code. It makes using a longer, more complex passcode easier because

Figure 6.4   Using Touch ID fingerprint recognition on an iOS device.

device owners will not have to enter it as frequently. Apple states, "Touch ID can be trained to recognize up to five different fingers. With one finger enrolled, the chance of a random match with someone else is 1 in 50,000." The keys needed for Touch ID to unlock the device are lost if the device reboots or after 48 hours; also, it only allows five failed attempts before the user must enter a passcode to unlock the device.

Touch ID can also be set up to approve on device purchases from the iTunes Store, the App Store, without entering an Apple ID password. Third-party apps can also use iOS system application programming interfaces (APIs) to ask the user to authenticate using Touch ID. For security purposes, the third-party app is only notified as to whether the authentication was successful. It is not allowed access to the Touch ID or the data stored with the enrolled fingerprint.

6.5.2 Android Biometrics

The variety of devices that utilize Android makes it difficult to implement hardware-specific features. The Android platform supports various biometric authentication hardware from a wide range of manufacturers. One of the first attempts at biometric authentication on Android was facial recognition. Starting with Android 4.1 Ice Cream Sandwich (Android tends to name its operating systems related to desserts and sweets), you could set your phone to unlock only when it sees your face. This feature, for obvious reasons, was not secure, as a printed photo of the device owner's face could have success unlocking a device.

Android also supports fingerprint authentication on supported devices. Android uses the fingerprint hardware abstraction layer to connect to fingerprint hardware. The fingerprint sensor of a device is usually dormant. But, in response to a call to authenticate, the fingerprint sensor waits for a scan. The user places a finger on the fingerprint sensor, and the vendor-specific library determines if there is a match based on the current set of enrolled templates, assuming that a fingerprint has been configured. As with Apple, fingerprint data are never accessible from outside the sensor driver or a Trusted Execution Environment; acquisition, enrollment, and recognition must occur here. Android system's API allows for third-party apps to interact directly with the fingerprint scanner.

Smart devices use a combination of hardware and software to combat the security challenges that the device users face in the modern-day world. In the next chapter, we will take a look at the other side with software and network services.

7

OPERATING SYSTEM SECURITY

7.1 Introduction

In Chapter 6, we discussed the security features of hardware in smart devices. This chapter will give you an overview of the security technologies and features that are implemented within the major smart device platform operating systems (OSs) currently in use. We will also discuss the network services that are available to the owners of smart devices and how these features enhance smart device security.

7.2 OS

OS security is the process put in place to protect the device from threats such as viruses, worms, malware, and hackers. OS security includes several preventive-control techniques, which protect any device assets that are capable of being compromised, modified, or destroyed. If an OS is accessed by an unauthorized user or other malicious entity, the consequences can be severe to the device and/or the data stored in it or that it has access to. An OS should be able to protect against unauthorized access, malicious access to system memory, viruses, worms, or other emerging threats to ensure that the OS is secure.

There are many steps to OS security that should be performed on a regular basis in a secure OS environment. For example, OS security could include performing regular OS security patch updates, regularly installing updated antivirus definitions and software updates, monitoring incoming and outgoing network traffic through a firewall, or maintaining secure accounts with secure privileges. New threats are discovered every day for computing devices. The security measures built in to the device have to step up to meet the ever-changing dangers that arise. It is paramount that all devices not only have strong security built into the device, but the OS should also ensure that the security is updated and maintained on a regular basis as needed.

In order to understand OS security for mobile devices, it is important to have a general idea of how all computing device OSs operate. An operating system is a program that initially loads into the device during its booting process. It manages all other programs that are installed or running on the device. The other programs on the device are referred to as applications or apps. Applications make use of the OS by making requests for services through the OS-defined application programming interface (API). Device users interact with the OS through a user interface (UI), such as a command language like disk operating system, or a graphical user interface (GUI) like Microsoft Windows.

The main function of the OS is to define how applications access the system's resources. The OS manages the device by controlling how hardware and software are used; the OS regulates how applications use the processor. The OS defines the means by which the application can access system resources. It is a buffer between applications and system hardware. It provides functionality for applications to access resources.

There are a number of different kinds of OSs, the most common are as follows:

1. *Real-time OS*—An OS is most often found in electronic equipment and other technical devices. Often, it requires very little user interaction or operation, aside from the initial configuration and subsequent changes. A real-time OS is intended to serve real-time application process data as they come in, usually without time delays. The processing time requirements (including any OS delay) are measured in tenths of seconds or shorter.

2. *Single-user single task system*—This OS was used by many early smart devices such as the early iPhones and PDA. This OS permits one user to operate only one application at a time. When a user wishes to use another application, the user must exit the previous running application before running a new one.

3. *Single-user multitasking system*—This OS is used by most modern smart devices and the extremely popular Microsoft Windows systems. In this environment, a user runs multiple applications and cycles through the various applications as he or she desires.

4. *Multiuser system*—A multiuser OS allows various users to operate a system's resources concurrently. An example of this type of system is Linux. In a Linux system, the OS can manage requests from various users.

The security measures that work for one type of OS environment may not function in another OS. It is important to understand which type of OS environment the device you are managing runs when evaluating the security of the device.

7.2.1 *Type of OS*

Apple's iOS, or iPhone OS as it was originally known, popularized the smart device market. There is no doubt that it is a major dominant force in the industry. Its main competitor in terms of device numbers is Android. It is important for smart device managers to be informed on the various OSs running smart devices and the companies behind them. The following is a list of the most popular smart device OSs:

1. *Android OS—Google Inc.:* The Android OS is Google's open and free software that consists of smart device OS, middleware, and smart device applications that run on smart devices, such as smartphones, tablets, and television set top boxes.
2. *iOS—Apple:* Apple's iOS, originally developed for iPhone devices, has branched to many smart devices; the OS now runs a number of Apple devices including the iPhone, iPad, iPod touch, and Apple TVs. The iOS mobile OS is available only on Apple's own manufactured devices as the company does not license the OS for third-party hardware.
3. *Windows Mobile/Windows Phone—Microsoft:* Windows Mobile/Windows Phone is Microsoft's mobile OS that is used in smartphones and other mobile devices. In the latest version, Microsoft plans to unify their smartphone platform with the Microsoft PC's OS and integrate it with other Microsoft services.
4. *Symbian OS—Nokia:* The Symbian OS is a mobile OS targeted at mobile phones that offers integration with communication and personal information management functionality. Symbian is widely used in low-end phones. Nokia has made

the Symbian platform available to platform development collaborators.

5. *BlackBerry OS—Research In Motion:* BlackBerry OS is a proprietary mobile OS developed by Research In Motion for use on the BlackBerry handheld and tablet devices. BlackBerry OS offers synchronization with Microsoft Exchange, Lotus Notes, and other popular email systems and connects with other popular business software that integrate well when used in conjunction with the BlackBerry Enterprise Server.

6. *Palm/Garnet OS—Palm, Inc.:* Palm OS is a proprietary mobile OS that has been around since 1996 on the Pilot 1000 handheld and later expanded to smart devices.

7. *WebOS (Palm/HP):* The WebOS is a mobile OS that runs on the Linux kernel. WebOS was developed as the successor to its Palm OS mobile OS. WebOS is a proprietary smart device OS. Acquired by HP, WebOS runs a number of devices including smartphones, tablets, smart watches and smart TVs.

8. *Bada—Samsung Electronics:* Bada is a proprietary mobile OS developed by Samsung. It was first launched in 2010. The Samsung Wave was the first smartphone to use this mobile OS.

9. *Firefox OS—Mozilla Foundation:* The Firefox OS was designed to be a complete, stand-alone OS for the open Web with a primary focus as an open-source mobile OS for mobile and tablet devices.

10. *Tizen OS—Linux Foundation, Tizen Association:* Tizen is an open-source, Linux-based OS, standards-based software platform for multiple device categories, including smartphones, tablets, and TVs.

Because Apple iOS and Android are, by far, the most popular, the focus of the rest of the chapters will be on these two OSs.

7.3 Authentication

Authentication is the action of identifying the user of the device and the associated executing applications with the user of the device. A secure OS environment should create a protective structure that ensures that the user who is running a particular program is positively authentic. The most popular forms of OS authentication of users are as follows:

1. *Username and password system*—A user must input a registered username and/or password with the OS to gain access to the system.
2. *Key system*—A user will need to punch a card in card slot or enter a key generated by the key generator provided by the OS to gain system access.
3. *Biometric system*—A user will need to verify their identity by means of a physical trait that is registered with the OS in order to gain access to the system.

Android and iOS OSs utilize advanced security features to protect the personal information stored. As with other popular OSs, a critical component of smart device security is passwords. Smart device passwords come in a variety of formats such as a pattern, a personal identification number (PIN), or the typical password. Most smart device users are familiar with a numeric PIN and an alphanumeric password, but they may not be familiar with pattern authentication. A pattern is a relatively new kind of password mostly used on Android that provides nine small dots in a square. By dragging your finger across at least four of them in a certain sequence, you can set up a pattern that must be retraced in order to unlock your device.

Whatever format you select, the function is the same; a person is required to know the pattern, PIN, or password to access the phone.

Once the passcode has been configured, Apple iOS and Android devices will automatically enable Data Protection or full disk encryption. iOS supports six-digit, four-digit, and arbitrary-length alphanumeric passcodes. Android supports this as well while also supporting pattern locks (see Figure 7.1). In addition to unlocking the device, a password provides access to certain encryption keys. This prevents an intruder in the possession of a device from getting access to data without the passcode. The stronger the user password is, the stronger the encryption key becomes. Device passwords are vulnerable to brute-force attacks. The larger and more complex the password, the more difficult it is to crack.

Most smart device users are opposed to typing large passwords every time they wish to access their device; that is why biometric

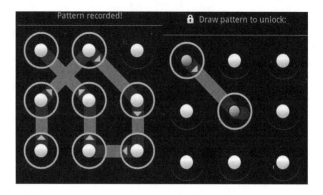

Figure 7.1   Pattern lock on an Android device.

features, such as fingerprint scanners, can assist users by allowing them to have a strong password and freeing them from the hassle of inputting it often. To defend against brute-force passcode attacks, most smart devices implement time delays after the entry of an incorrect password at the lock screen. Other features exist that will erase all data on the device automatically after a specified number of consecutive incorrect attempts to enter the password.

7.4 Application Security

Third-party applications (or apps) are a major reason for the success of smart devices. This can be viewed not only as a blessing but also as a curse. Many apps provide amazing experience and benefits for the user, but there is also the potential for an app to harm the device's security and performance or perhaps compromise user data. For this reason, third-party apps must be handled with care. It is important for smart device platforms to provide multiple layers of protection to ensure that apps are safe for the user.

One layer of protection to app security is code signing, which is the procedure of digitally signing applications to confirm that the software author can ensure that the code has not been modified or corrupted since it was signed by the use of a cryptographic hash. For iOS, it is mandatory that all apps come from a known and approved source and have not been tampered with; this requires that all executable codes be signed using an Apple-issued certificate. Therefore, all third-party apps must also be validated and signed using an Apple-issued certificate. Android prohibits installing an unsigned code by default but can be configured to run the unsigned code through the configuration settings.

In order to develop and install apps on iOS devices, developers must register with Apple and join the iOS Developer Program. The real-world identity of each developer, whether an individual or a business, is verified by Apple before their certificate is issued. This certificate enables developers to sign apps and submit them to the App Store for distribution. For Android, this is not necessary; because Android is an open platform, anyone with a computer can develop an application and actually run it on a device. The identity verification makes it less likely that a person will try to commit a malicious act for the fear of facing legal consequences.

An *app marketplace* is a type of digital distribution platform for software application (often for smart devices). There is only one legitimate marketplace for applications in the iOS environment: *Apple's App Store*. There are a number of Android marketplaces; the most popular ones are the *Google Play* and the *Amazon Appstore*. iOS apps have to be reviewed by Apple to ensure that they operate as described and do not contain obvious bugs or other problems. The Google Play Store requires no review, but other Android marketplaces such as Amazon do mandate a review. The mandatory review process, in addition to other app security measures, allows consumers to be confident that the apps they download are safe.

7.5 Permissions

iOS and Android make use of a permission system that allows the user to access the personal data or services of the smart devices. On Android, no application has permission to perform an operation that could negatively affect other applications, the OS, or the user. If an app wishes to have access to things like contacts, Internet access, or the device's camera hardware, the app must declare that it will have permissions to do so, and then the user must accept that permission before the app can be installed. To install an app, a user is presented with a list of permissions that the application is declaring.

On both platforms, an application must ask the user to grant these permissions to the app in order to access certain features on the device. See Tables 7.1 and 7.2 for iOS and Android permissions.

Table 7.1 iOS Entitlements

Contacts	READ_CONTACTS
	WRITE_CONTACTS
Microphone	RECORD_AUDIO
Calendars	READ_CALENDAR
	WRITE_CALENDAR
Camera	CAMERA ACCESS
Reminders	READ_ REMINDERS
	WRITE_ REMINDERS
HomeKit	ACCESS TO HOMEKIT SERVICE
Photos	ACCESS TO SAVED PHOTOS
HealthKit	ACCESS TO HEALTHKIT SERVICE
Location	ACCESS TO LOCATION SERVICE

Table 7.2 Android Permissions

Calendar	READ_CALENDAR
	WRITE_CALENDAR
CAMERA	CAMERA
CONTACTS	READ_CONTACTS
	WRITE_CONTACTS
	GET_ACCOUNTS
LOCATION	ACCESS_FINE_LOCATION
	ACCESS_COARSE_LOCATION
MICROPHONE	RECORD_AUDIO
PHONE	READ_PHONE_STATE
	CALL_PHONE
	READ_CALL_LOG
	WRITE_CALL_LOG
	ADD_VOICEMAIL
	USE_SIP
	PROCESS_OUTGOING_CALLS
SENSORS	BODY_SENSORS
SMS	SEND_SMS
	RECEIVE_SMS
	READ_SMS
	RECEIVE_WAP_PUSH
	RECEIVE_MMS
STORAGE	READ_EXTERNAL_STORAGE
	WRITE_EXTERNAL_STORAGE
NFC	NFC
INTERNET	INTERNET

iOS takes a different approach. iOS asks a user the first time an app requests to utilize a particular feature. For instance, the first time you use the Google Maps app on an Apple smart device, the application will ask if you would like to grant this application access to your current location (Figure 7.2a). From the settings menu, these permissions can be adjusted at any time.

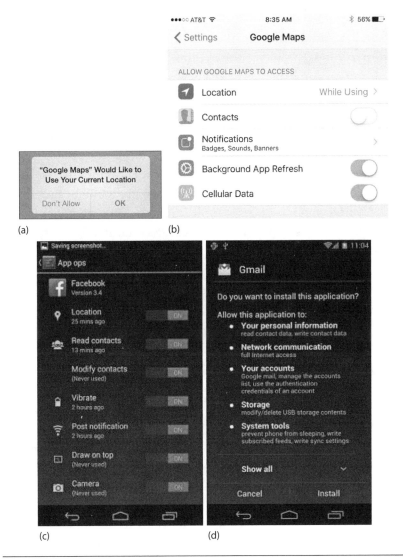

(a)   (b)

(c)   (d)

Figure 7.2   iOS and Android permissions. (a) Request to view your location in iOS; iOS (b) and Android; (c) settings for App permission; and (d) Android permission request on install.

Android has a long list of permissions and controls that are far more granularly defined than iOS (Figure 7.2c). For instance, an application could have read access to your contacts but not have write access to your contacts. Here is an example of the more important permissions that contain sensitive data.

7.6 Application Sandbox

iOS and Android make use of an Application Sandbox. This isolates third-party app data and code execution from other apps and prevents them from making changes to the device.

In iOS, each app has a unique home directory for its files, which is randomly assigned when the app is installed. If a third-party app needs to access information other than its own, it does so only by using the services provided by the iOS platform. The Android platform uses a Linux user-based system for identifying and isolating application resources. An Android device assigns a unique user ID to each Android application and runs it as that user in a separate process.

This approach is different from other OSs such as Windows, where multiple applications run with the same user permissions. Android has a kernel-level Application Sandbox. The kernel imposes security between applications and the system at the process level through standard Linux facilities, such as user and group IDs that are assigned to applications. Applications are unable to access other applications. If an application attempts to do something malicious like reading another app's data or dialing the phone without permission, the Android OS will prevent this based on the application's privileges.

System files and resources are also shielded from the user's apps.

On iOS, all third-party apps function as a nonprivileged user. The OS is read-only to prevent malicious modification from a rogue application. Access to third-party apps or user information and features, such as iCloud, is controlled using declared entitlements. Entitlements are key value pairs that are signed in to an app and allow authentication. These entitlements are digitally signed, and they cannot be modified.

Entitlements are used by system applications to perform specific privileged operations that would otherwise require elevated permissions to accomplish. Apps must perform background processing through system

APIs that are provided by the iOS platform. In order for apps to inter-act with each other, iOS allows what is called extensions. Extensions are special-purpose signed executable binaries, packaged within an app. The iOS system can detect an extension when the app is installed. It then makes this extension available to other apps using a matching system. Extensions are sandboxed like any other third-party app, and they have their own container that is separate from the master app's container. They do share the same permissions as the container app. For instance, if a user grants camera access to an app, this permission will be extended to the extensions that belong to the app.

7.7 Network Services

The rise of smart devices has brought the cloud to millions of users. Current smart devices are seamlessly integrated with the cloud. Network services can minimize smart devices' resource consumption by leveraging vast cloud resources. Cloud servers can perform more complex functions while drastically reducing smart device resources' usage.

Cloud integration allows smartphones to perform functions such as backup and recovery, finding lost devices, and centralizing file storage. The possibilities are truly endless. Sometimes, it is far more efficient to perform a function on a remote server than on a local device. The cloud can store a user's contacts, calendars, photos, and documents and keeps the information up to date across all of his or her devices, automatically. Smart devices have a natural limitation in computing power, disk space, and battery life; this makes it difficult for smart devices to perform some needed security functions on the device. Using a combination of cloud and local resources allows the smart devices to maintain and increase functionality and security.

7.7.1 *iCloud*

Apple iOS devices use a service called iCloud; users set up iCloud by signing in with an Apple ID and choosing which services they would like to use. iCloud has features such as *My Photo Stream* (a photo synchronization service across devices), iCloud Drive (cen-tralized file storage), and Backup (cloud backup service). If the smart device manager of an organization deems any of these listed services as unsuitable for corporate activity, these services can be disabled by information technology administrators via a configuration profile.

One of the most important security features available to iOS device owners and administrators is the *Find My iPhone* cloud service for the remote location-tracking of iOS devices and Mac computers (Figure 7.3). This service allows users to locate their iOS devices via the iOS app or on the iCloud Website (http://www.icloud.com). This service allows users to do the following:

- *Play Sound*—Makes the device play a sound at maximum volume and makes flashing on screen even if it is muted. This feature is useful if the device has been misplaced.
- *Lost Mode (iOS 6 or later)*—Flags the device as lost or stolen, allowing the user to lock it with a passcode. If the device is an iPhone, and someone finds the device, they can call the user directly on the device.
- *Erase iPhone*—Completely erases all content and settings. This is useful if the device contains sensitive information, but the device cannot be located after this action is performed. Starting with iOS 7 or later, after the erase is complete, the message can still be displayed, and the device will be activation-locked. This makes it hard for someone to use or sell the device should the owner of the device misplace it. An Apple ID Password will be required before turning off Find My iPhone, signing out of iCloud, erasing the device, or reactivating a device after a remote wipe.

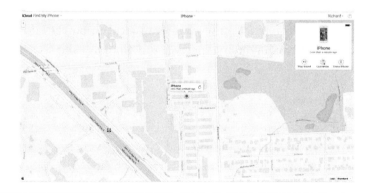

Figure 7.3 Find My iPhone application.

Figure 7.4   Android Device Manager application.

7.7.2 *Android Device Manager*

On the other side, Android has a similar cloud application called the Android Device Manager (Figure 7.4). It is a Google app that allows you to track and secure your devices remotely. Depending on the permissions you have given the Android Device Manager in the Google Settings app, you can remotely track your devices, cause them to ring (even if it was put in silent mode), change the lock code, or completely wipe your devices.

New functions, including the ability to ring or text your missing device, have recently been added so that, if someone finds your phone, you can get in touch with them and ask them to return the device.

iOS and Android devices can be erased remotely by an administrator or a user. A remote wipe command can be initiated by mobile device management, Exchange, Android Device Manager, or iCloud. When a remote wipe command is triggered, the device sends a confirmation and performs the wipe. When a remote wipe command is initiated via Exchange, the device will check in with the Exchange Server before performing the wipe.

7.8 Jailbreaking/Rooting

Jailbreaking and rooting are often used interchangeably but are, in fact, very different. Jailbreaking and rooting are methods that will give you unrestricted or administrative access to your mobile device's entire file system. This offers a greater amount of control and the ability to customize the device. Greater control sounds great, but this can open the device to risk. Often, these custom modifications have not been adequately tested. Circumventing the imposed restrictions of the platform is dangerous and may open the device to huge security risks.

The term jailbreaking refers to Apple iOS devices including iPhone, iPad, Apple TV, etc., whereas rooting refers to Android devices. Jailbreaking is eliminating the restrictions that Apple placed on its devices to run the iOS OS. When you jailbreak, you start the device with a custom kernel, and it gives the user root access to the device. A jailbroken device can download third-party apps that are not available in the App Store. These devices can use extensions and themes that are not Apple approved. The iOS device functions normally for the most part as you still have access to all the normal iOS functions and services unless changed.

Rooting is quite different; unlike iOS devices, Android users can run third-party apps from the start. It is important to note that Android is an open system, whereas Apple iOS is very much a closed one. Normally, on Android devices, the kernel and some core applications run with root permissions. Root access has the full control of all applications and all application data. A rooted Android device can grant root access to any application; this increases the security risk of malicious applications. Some people have a legitimate reason for modifying their Android system, such as developers. Developers often use this access to install different OSs for the purposes of testing applications and the system. Rooting your Android device can improve performance.

Often, Android device manufacturers ship devices with a larger number of unwanted applications to the end user that may slow down performance. Sometimes, custom read-only memories can provide far better performance as they are not burdening this limitation. Rooted apps can also perform actions such as overclocking the phone's processor.

As stated earlier in this section, jailbreaking and rooting a smart device are dangerous. When performing the action of jailbreaking or rooting, there is always the chance of rendering your device inoperable. When managing a smart device, remember that these modified devices can compromise the security and reliability of the platform.

Just like a computer, smart devices are vulnerable to malware similar to a laptop or desktop system. The advantage of getting apps only from an official marketplace reduces the chance that a device would be exposed to malicious code. Jailbreaking/rooting could also limit your ability to get service or support of the device. Some manufacturers will void the warranty if the device has been jailbroken or rooted.

8
SECURING SMART DEVICES

8.1 Recommended Methodology

Most organizations deployed BlackBerry devices for corporate use to access email and provide messaging for their employees. These organizations knew that the security provided by the BlackBerry Enterprise Server complied with their security policies. A few years ago, a genius named Steve Jobs changed all that. He announced devices like iPads and iPhones. And, of course, Google was not going to be left behind. They made their Android OS available to phone manufacturers for nothing.

With the advent of these smart devices like iPads, iPhones, and Android phones, organizations are searching for a secure solution for these devices similar to the one that they have for their BlackBerry devices. A term called MDM originated. MDM stands for mobile device management. Several vendors have developed solutions to assist organizations in managing their smart devices.

Typically, information technology (IT) organizations are chartered to manage these devices. Before they select the MDM solution, they must engage the key departments within the organization to understand the planned usage of these smart devices and gather requirements. Most IT organizations are surprised when they hear the marketing department on how they are planning to use the smart devices, or, better yet, hear how the chief executive officer or the chief financial officer is planning to utilize the newly acquired iPad.

We suggest a 10-step approach for organizations. We call this approach the PIM approach (Figure 8.1). PIM stands for plan–implement–manage.

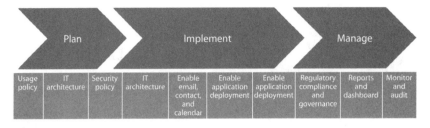

Figure 8.1 Managing smart devices using PIM—Plan, Implement, Monitor.

Step 1: During the acceptable use policy development, several questions should be asked and answered by key departments within the organization. These questions help identify the requirements and provide input into the next step of defining the IT architecture. It helps to identify the right solutions after asking the right questions. The questions are like the following:

- Do you want to allow corporate devices or to bring your own device?
- Is there a separation of personal versus corporate data on your device?
- Is your device intended only for corporate use or for both corporate and personal use? Can you play Angry Bird on your device?
- Is there an agreement with employees to abide by corporate security policies (e.g., remote wipe, or a record of their phone calls may be viewed by corporate)?
- Would confidential data be allowed on smart devices, and how will they be monitored and controlled?
- What type of smart devices will be allowed? Apple only? Android only? Or limited by operating systems?
- How are you going to manage the backup?
- Would you want the device to connect to the corporate network?
- Which apps would you like to deploy? Corporate apps? Own marketplace?

Step 2: Once the answers to these questions have been obtained, a draft IT architecture should be designed to support the deployment of an MDM solution. For example, an answer to the question "Corporate device versus personal device?" may imply whether an organization can wipe out the entire device if it is lost or if they need a secure *container* within the device to house the corporate data.

The IT architecture may also address questions such as the following:

- Cloud-based solution versus internally deployed?
- Hosted versus self-supported?
- Scalability and performance issues based on the number of devices?
- How will the current IT architecture support the mobile architecture?

Step 3: Once the requirements have been defined and the supporting IT architecture has been designed, the security policies to support the mobile strategy should be developed. The security policy may address some or all of these questions:

- Password policy control
- Encryption requirements
- Port control (Wi-fi, Bluetooth, camera)
- Remote lock/unlock/wipe
- Asset tracking
- Device configuration (virtual private network [VPN], email, Wi-fi)
- Delivery and control of applications to the device
- Blacklisting/whitelisting
- Audit and monitoring

Step 4: Now, you start to use the requirements that were identified during the planning phase and select the right MDM solution. The implementation of the IT architecture is completed, and the proof of concept (PoC) or pilot implementation is completed. Typically, a select few devices are managed under the PoC or pilot implementation. The following steps are executed:

- Emails are identified for the selected device owners.
- A self-registry link is sent to the users.
- Users enter the registry information and obtain credentials.
- Security policies are pushed down on the device.
- The device is ready for use.

Step 5: Enable the email, contact, and calendar features according to the mobile architecture and policies that are defined during the planning phase. Typically, organizations combine the features available within the ActiveSync/Lotus Notes features with the features in the selected MDM solution. This step brings the same functions that are available in BlackBerry to the smart devices. At a minimum, organizations should enable the email, contact, and calendar features.

Step 6: Within this step, organizations roll out custom mobile applications to the smart devices. There are several decisions that you probably made during the planning phase. You probably answered the following questions during the planning phase:

- Are you going to have your own marketplace from where your employees can download applications?
- Are you going to develop applications for the Apple platform, the Android platform, or both?
- Are most of the applications going to be browser-based applications, or will they be native custom mobile applications?
- Will employees download these applications from the Apple and/or Android marketplace?
- Are you going to develop these applications in-house, or will a third party develop these applications for you?

During this step, you will need two major processes:

1. *Ability to verify that the source code is written based on the guidelines provided by the Open Web Application Security Project.* These include requiring appropriate source code analysis tools and the ability to perform penetration testing of the application.
2. *To incorporate your corporate systems development life cycle (SDLC) process in the development of mobile applications.*

In some cases, we have seen organizations that are lax in meeting the requirements.

Step 7: During this step, smart devices begin to act like a laptop and can remotely connect to the corporate network and access corporate resources like servers, local area network shared drives, and other corporate data. The focus during this step is to ensure that the same rugged security features are deployed as they are for your remote laptop connection. You should look into your remote access policy to ensure that it supports the connection of smart devices to the corporate network.

VPN configuration, encryption parameters, and virtualization concepts may come into play as you deploy the right solution for this step.

Step 8: During this step, appropriate measures are taken to ensure that the implemented solution complies with the regulatory requirements of the Sarbanes–Oxley Act (SOX), the Health Insurance Portability and Accountability Act, the Payment Card Industry, and others. If the smart device is going to contain financial data, personal health data, personally identifiable information, or credit card information (and, most likely, you will if you store emails on your smart device), these data must be secured. In addition, the installed mobile solution must have the ability to produce appropriate reports to satisfy the audit requirements of these regulations.

Step 9: This step is to provide adequate support to monitor and report on the managed devices. The examples of the type of reports include the following:

- The number of devices supported and an inventory of the devices
- The current location of each device
- The number of remote wipes performed in a month/quarter/year
- The number of stolen or lost devices

Step 10: This step provides the necessary support to internal/external auditors when they perform their audits. More and more of the auditors are targeting the audit of smart devices as they are beginning to agree that the smart devices are becoming the *weakest link* of their security program.

8.2 Other Considerations

Some of the other considerations related to smart devices may include the following:

- *e-Discovery:* You should evaluate your current e-Discovery process to see if smart devices need to be included in this process.
- *Litigation hold:* During the litigation process, it may become important to include smart devices during litigation hold.
- *Export control laws:* If your organization deals with certain technologies that have export control requirements, you may want to track the smart devices to ensure that the device is not in the countries where export control laws may be violated.

PART III

MANAGING SMART DEVICES

This section will operationalize the plan–implement–manage (PIM) methodology that is introduced in Chapter 8 of Part II. The PIM methodology is a framework that every organization can use to manage smart devices. Each step of the PIM methodology takes you through a structured approach of securing and managing smart devices.

So, let's get started.

9

Smart Device Use Policy

9.1 Introduction

Every organization must have a smart device use policy. This does not have to be a separate document, as the use policy for smart devices can be incorporated in an existing use policy document. But, whether you have a separate smart device use policy, or the use policy of smart devices is embedded into another use policy, it must address how the smart devices will be allowed for usage within the organization. Before the use policy is finalized, the following should be considered:

1. Will the organization ask the employee to sign an agreement before the device is issued to the employee?
2. Will the organization support personally owned devices (or bring your own device [BYOD], as explained in Part I)? Or will the organization provide the employees with a device? Or will the organization support a combination of personally owned and corporate-owned devices?
3. Will the organization reimburse the employees for their device if used for the organization?
4. Will the organization support all types of devices? Just Apple devices? Android devices? Microsoft devices? Or how about the BlackBerry devices?

Let us take each of these considerations and discuss them in a little more detail.

9.2 Smart Device Use Agreement

Before any device is issued to an employee or a contractor (where it is owned by the employee or the employer), a smart device user agreement should be signed by the employee. This agreement should be in place prior to any synchronization that takes place between the device and the employer information systems environment. The following points should be addressed in the agreement:

- *That the employee agrees to follow all the employer's policies related to the use of smart devices.*
- *That the employer will enforce the settings on the device that may limit the use of the device.* These limitations may include, but are not limited to, the enforcement of password policies, network connection protocols, and encryption enforcement.
- *That the employer may wipe out all information on the smart device in case it is lost or stolen, including any personal data that may reside on the device.* It is the responsibility of the employee to make appropriate backups of the data on the smart device. In that way, the employee does not hold the employer liable in case the personal data are accidentally erased.
- *That the employee agrees to not copy or move the corporate data from the device without the knowledge of the employer.*
- *That any attempt made by the employee to modify the underlying operating system (OS) of the device ("rooting" or "jailbreaking") will be interpreted as a violation of this agreement, and the device will be immediately disconnected from the employer's information systems.*
- *That the employee agrees to use only the approved tools and methods that are provided by the employer to handle any sensitive employer information (e.g., protected health information [PHI] and personally identifiable information [PII] or any other information identified by the employer as sensitive).*
- *That the employee agrees to notify the employer of lost or stolen device (e.g., employer's help desk) immediately or within the time allowed by the employer's policy.*
- *That the employer may (in some cases) use Global Positioning System signals to locate the employee.*
- *That the employee understands that failure to adhere to this agreement or failure to appropriately protect the smart device could result in action against the employee, including the termination*

of employment, civil action, or criminal prosecution by the affected
persons (e.g., if the PHI or PII information is disclosed by a cus-
tomer of the employer or another employee).

9.3 BYOD or Not?

It is the opinion of the authors that most information technology
(IT) organizations are under pressure to produce more for less. The
IT budgets are under pressure, and the chief information officer
(CIO) is constantly looking to reduce the infrastructure budgets.
The concepts of cloud computing and BYOD are two such examples where the CIO is looking to reduce its infrastructure costs by
(1) moving the infrastructure into a cloud environment where the
infrastructure is shared among different users and (2) allowing the
employees to bring their own devices (BYOD) to reduce the cost of
the smart devices.

It is also understandable that the employees typically will have
newer devices than those the employer can provide to the employee.
Therefore, the employee is actually happier to use their own device
as not only is it newer, but they are also familiar with how to use the
device.

It is the authors' opinion that most organizations have adopted the
BYOD for most or some of their employees and that majority of the
organizations have a hybrid environment where they provide some
employer-owned devices (e.g., to executives) and allow BYOD for the
general employees.

9.4 Reimbursement of Smart Devices

It is a common practice for employers to reimburse the employee for
the monthly expenses that are charged by the service provider. The
employers, in some cases, have arranged for the service provider themselves and made them available to the employees (e.g., agreement with
key service providers like Verizon, AT&T, Sprint, and T-Mobile). In
other cases, the employee selects the service provider and submits a
monthly expense reimbursement request.

The process in which the employer requests the employee for reimbursement can be a subject of debate. The question is the details that are required by the employer from the employee prior to any reimbursement. These details could be in the form of a monthly invoice listing all the expenses charged by the service provider. In a BYOD environment, this may be a concern to an employee if they have to submit the details of all their phone calls made during a given month, assuming that there may be personal calls, and the employee may not want the employer to know all their personal phone numbers.

9.5 Types of Supported OS

There is always a debate in organizations as to which OSs to support in case of a BYOD environment. If the devices are provided by the employer, it is an easier decision for the employer (like the case during BlackBerry days). But, in a BYOD environment, there is a very good possibility that the BYOD devices will have different OSs (commonly used OSs like Apple, Android, Windows, and BlackBerry and some less commonly used OSs like Symbian, Palm OS, Bada, Open WebOS, Maemo, and MeeGo).

The key consideration for employers is to ensure that the OSs they support have the necessary security features. For example, as discussed in Chapter 7, the earlier versions of Android OS did not have robust security features, whereas the later versions do have those features. So, if the employer draws a line as to which OSs are supported, and which versions of the supported OS are allowed, it becomes a concern for those employees who do not want to change their BYOD device and do not want to incur additional expenses to buy another device.

9.6 Other Considerations

Many organizations allow their service providers (IT vendors, consultants, and others) to synchronize with the corporate email. It is our opinion that the organization must use the same rigor and agreements for the service providers as they use for the employees.

It is also suggested that the agreements are made with not only the service providers but also the employees of the service providers (unless the service provider can provide evidence that they have a process in place to manage the BYOD environment of their employees).

10

SECURITY POLICY

10.1 Introduction

Every organization must define a security policy for smart devices. This policy should outline the security features that must be configured on every smart device that contains corporate information. The policy should be defined based on the types of usage of the smart device. For example, if the organization plans to only access email using a smart device, the device can be configured with a limited set of security features, whereas, if the smart device will connect to the corporate network (like a laptop), then additional security considerations may be deployed on the device. These decisions should be made at an organization level, not at an individual smart device level, to make the deployment of the policy easier.

The security policy, at a minimum, should address the following features and functionalities:

- Password policy control
- Encryption requirements
- Port control (Wi-fi, Bluetooth, camera)
- Remote lock/unlock/wipe
- Asset tracking
- Device configuration (Virtual Private Network [VPN], email, Wi-fi)
- The delivery and control of applications to the device
- Blacklisting/whitelisting
- Audit and monitoring

Let us take each one of these and discuss it in more detail.

10.2 Password Policy Control

It is probably obvious to the majority of readers that the password is the first line of defense in protecting information on smart devices. If a user does not use a password, or uses a trivial password, they just make it easier for a hacker or someone who finds your lost smart device to gain access to the information residing on the smart device.

Organizations must define a password policy for all smart devices that contain their data. Common sense would dictate that organizations carry over the same password policy that they have for their corporate environment to the smart device world. But the implementation of such a policy on smart devices could prove to be impractical. One reason is that the type and size of a keyboard differs from those of a desktop or a laptop. The full function of a keyboard is usually not available on a single screen of a smart device. Toggling the keyboard through two or three different screens to enter a password can be cumbersome.

So, if organizations have a complex password requirement for their desktop and laptop (e.g., upper case, lower case, special characters etc.), they may look into enforcing a longer alphabet password but not requiring the need for numeric, upper case, lower case, or special characters. As security practitioners, we believe that this compromise is an acceptable risk.

We suggest the following as a minimum requirement for password policy:

- Minimum of six characters
- Do not allow consecutive characters or duplicate characters (e.g., "aaaaaa" or "111111" or "123456")
- Force the change of passwords every 180 days

Of course, if your organization has an appetite for a stronger password, then you are ahead of the password game.

10.3 Encryption

Both hardware manufacturers and software developers have made great strides in tackling the encryption topic and making the smart device content more secure. For example, the Apple iOS operating system has started to encrypt all data at rest with version 8 and higher.

In terms of configuring the encryption features of your smart device, organizations should determine the type of use of the device and deploy the appropriate configuration requirements. For example, if the device will be connected to the corporate network, the appropriate features of *data in motion* and *data in use* should be deployed.

10.4 Port Control

This section will cover three different ports: (1) Wi-fi, (2) Bluetooth, and (3) camera. All these ports can potentially pose some risks to organizations. For example, allowing cameras to be used in a smart device could allow users to take pictures of sensitive drawings from a research organization, or allowing the use of Wi-fi or Bluetooth can open up the potential possibility of a hacker eavesdropping the communication.

Although these ports are useful for employees, organizations must consider the risks associated with these ports and decide in their security policy whether they will allow the use of these ports. Some organizations are starting to use the geolocation capabilities of the smart devices to determine whether these ports can be used or not. For example, an organization may decide that, if the user is in a technology building, the cameras may be used, but, if the user is in the research building, the cameras will be turned off. Another example is that an organization may turn off the Wi-fi or Bluetooth of a smart device if the user is not in the corporate facility.

10.5 Remote Lock/Unlock and Wipe

The probability is very high that the employees of your organization will sooner or later either lose or misplace a smart device. As part of your use policy, it should be expected that the user will notify the organization within a reasonable time frame that the device has been lost or stolen. The ability for an organization to remote lock/unlock or wipe the device is probably the most important feature of the security policy.

Most organizations use Microsoft Exchange and utilize the ActiveSync feature of Exchange to synchronize the email between the Exchange server and the smart device. This ActiveSync has the ability to remotely lock and unlock devices and wipe the device, if necessary.

The security policy should address the duration for which the organization would lock the device (in case the device is later found by the employee) and the duration after which the organization will wipe the device.

Of course, if you are using a mobile device management software, it will have the capabilities of performing the unlocking/locking/wiping of the device as well.

10.6 Asset Tracking

Organizations have the ability to track smart devices by utilizing the geolocation feature of the smart device. Most hardware and software in the smart device provide organizations this ability. The decision to make is whether the organizations want to track the asset on a routine basis and whether the employees feel comfortable allowing the organizations to monitor their whereabouts at all times.

At a minimum, the security policy should address an organization's stance on whether they will track assets and, if so, at what times. It will also be necessary to identify the type of information that they will collect and how the data will be used. (For example, would the organization use the data to keep track of employee's activities, or are they purely utilized to track the smart device?)

10.7 Device Configuration

An organization must plan on how the smart devices will be used within the organization. If the device will be connecting to the corporate network, the organization must define the appropriate policy for the smart device to connect to the corporate network. This could be in the form of a VPN or a virtual desktop.

10.8 Application Control and Proliferation

If an organization is planning to push an application to smart devices, they have several ways of doing it. A security policy defines the protocol of which applications are allowed and which ones are not critical to make sure that the user of smart devices only executes secure applications. The easiest way for an organization would be to establish their own marketplace or application store, where users can go and download corporate-approved apps.

10.9 Blacklisting/Whitelisting

An organization can also define a policy that identifies all the approved applications (whitelisted) that can be loaded on a smart device. Any applications that are not in the whitelisted table are not allowed to be downloaded on the smart device. This is a restrictive approach to applications.

If an organization does not want to deal with whitelisting, they can define a policy that identifies all the applications that are not allowed (blacklisted) to be run on the smart device. This is a prohibitive approach to applications.

11

MOBILE DEVICE MANAGEMENT

11.1 Introduction

The industry term, mobile device management (MDM), is used to describe the administration of smart devices via many types of access control and monitoring technologies. Mostly used in reference to the organizational use of smart devices, that permits an organization to allow business-related data to be stored and accessed on these devices while protecting these resources from unauthorized access. The bring-your-own-device (BYOD) trend has forced the hand of organizations; they now have to take a good, hard look at their approach to smart device security in their organizations.

Most MDM solutions contain a server that manages the smart devices and a client side application or service that is located on the smart device. The client receives commands from the server. MDM is a way to ensure that employees stay productive and do not breach corporate policies. Many organizations control the smart device activities of their employees using MDM products/services. Using an MDM solution, organizations can do the following:

- Ensure that the device password meets the defined requirements
- Ensure corporate data separation
- Secure emails
- Securely distribute corporate documents on a smart device
- Implement and enforce a smart device policy
- Perform a remote wipe (removal of data) of corporate or all data stored on the device
- Detect jailbroken or rooted devices
- Remote-lock a device

- Disable native features or apps on the device
- Ensure that system security updates are installed

In order to determine the correct MDM solution, an evaluator must have an understanding of the different features available. MDM solutions can come in a variety of formats, offer diverse features, and have varied platform support. Solutions may be either self-hosted by the organization or software as a cloud-based service.

11.2 Containerize or Noncontainerize?

There are two main approaches that MDM solutions employ to manage smart devices and protect data. These two approaches can be referred to as (1) containerization and (2) noncontainerization.

A solution that takes the containerized approach will reserve a small portion of storage to the MDM application on the smart device, segregating all corporate data, apps, and data transmission to this containerized area.

In a containerized solution, the personal data from a smart device will not be integrated into the MDM container, and the container will ensure that its data do not mingle with personal data. With a containerized solution, if a smart device is ever lost or compromised, a remote wipe of the containerized portion on the smart device will remove all the data stored without the worry of removing the device owner's precious personal data. The downside of a containerized MDM is that users must use the MDM-created applications to access their data, instead of the variety of applications that run on that platform. Users will not be able to leverage new features or applications that are available to the platform for corporate access, unless implemented by the MDM vendor.

Noncontainerized MDM solutions permit users to use their smart device with the native applications and features available to the platform of their choosing. This includes the access of corporate and personal data defined by the MDM policy. In this approach, MDM administrators can control personal and business applications. In a noncontainerized environment, it can be difficult to determine where sensitive data reside on the device as opposed to personal data. In this situation, when a device is lost or stolen, or an employee leaves the organization, it is difficult to wipe business data without harming personal data.

11.3 MDM Features

Now that you understand the different approaches to MDM methodologies, let us explain how some of the various features of an MDM solution can protect your organization.

11.3.1 Remote Wipe

A remote wipe function is available natively on the majority of smart devices through Exchange ActiveSync (EAS), MDM solutions, and consumer cloud apps such as Apple's *Find My iPhone*.

A remote wipe is one of the most essential features in an MDM solution for securing smart devices. It allows the MDM administrator or the device owner to send a command to a smart device and remove data. A remote wipe of a smart device is usually performed to keep information from falling into the wrong hands. This ensures that the sensitive information on a smart device can no longer be accessed, as it no longer resides on the device.

There are many different types of remote wipes, such as the following:

- *Complete factory reset*—The removal of all settings, user data, applications, and stored app data from a smart device's internal storage. This restores the device to factory condition.
- *Complete device wipe*—This destroys all the data stored on the smart device's system partition. This removes the keys that are used to encrypt everything in the partition, rather than erasing the storage partition.
- *Selective wipe*—Removes the specific device settings, user-created data, applications, and stored app data that the MDM solution manages on the device. This will remove all the MDM-installed applications, data, and the configurations that are pushed down by the MDM solution. This could also remove business emails while leaving the user's personal email untouched. Things like messages, or other data associated with business applications, can also be removed.

- *Container removal*—This will uninstall the secure container on the device and the data stored in it. One of the benefits of a secure container is that the administrator knows exactly where the business data reside, and most containers do a good job of preventing data leakage to the other areas of the smart device.

11.3.2 Password Enforcement

Some smart device users do not set up a personal identification number (PIN) or a password security. If employees are allowed access to sensitive business data, an organization should confirm that all the smart devices have an active password or PIN protecting their device. Password enforcement is essential to protecting smart devices. MDM solutions can push down a policy to enforce a PIN or a passcode to smart devices. An active password or PIN will keep a smart device safe from unauthorized individuals who obtain a lost or stolen device.

11.3.3 Application Control

An MDM solution can control what applications can be installed on the device and control system updates that can be applied. Whitelisted apps can be used to ensure that all applications on the device are authorized and cannot harm the device or the organization's network. It can also ensure that the application is appropriate to use on the device.

For instance, you may want to make sure that the users are unable to play games on corporate devices. The available applications can vary from user to user, group, or device. The applications available to users or devices can be defined by job function. Application control can also ensure that all cameras are disabled on smart devices (if that is what is required by an organization's policy). Organizations can ensure that malicious applications are not running on devices that could damage their security.

11.3.4 Jailbreak or Root Detection

Jailbreaking or rooting is a great risk to any organization's security. A rooted or jailbroken smart device weakens the built-in security features of the smart device platform. It allows a user to access the device's system to perform functions that could be unsafe. It is important for an MDM solution to detect and alert administrators when a device is rooted or jailbroken.

11.3.5 Encryption

Organizations should ensure that all sensitive data stored on smart devices are encrypted. A device that does not support the required ability to perform the necessary encryptions should not be allowed any access. An MDM solution can be used to ensure that a device is encrypted and that encryption is configured on all smart devices. Encryption protects the smart device and the data stored on it.

11.3.6 Other MDM Features

There are a number of MDM features that can greatly benefit an organization. MDM solutions can preconfigure a virtual private network (VPN), Wi-fi, and business email among other things. With an MDM solution, organizations can securely configure systems without having to distribute this information to employees and assist them with the setup. The configurations can be pushed down to the device by MDM once the device is registered to MDM.

Some MDM solutions can limit access to restricted Websites. This allows them to enact a policy to keep the users' browsing experience secure as defined by the organization's policy.

MDM solutions also have a feature that is called geofencing, which allows an organization to enforce different policies on a smart device based on the device's geographical location. For instance, with geofencing, you could allow employees the ability to use their camera only when they are not in sensitive areas. Geofencing is very difficult to implement and define as employees tend to move around a lot. It should only be used if your organization has a policy regarding geofencing.

11.4 Microsoft EAS

Exchange ActiveSync is a protocol that is used to communicate between mobile device email clients and Microsoft Exchange Server.

It supports many different device management features and policies—the most important being password requirements, encryption, remote wiping, and reporting device information.

While EAS works well in a lot of cases, it has some drawbacks. For example, not all devices support all of the settings. On iOS devices, EAS can do slightly more advanced things like disabling the browser or restricting the use of a camera. The Apple Website provides a full list of EAS features that are supported by iOS.

Android is similar, but, unfortunately, it is always a little bit more difficult to know what is supported with so many different device configurations floating around. The basic difference is that Android does not allow the disabling of the browser.

One of the most widely used tools for maintaining smart device security is Microsoft Exchange ActiveSync. Many information technology (IT) departments have been utilizing ActiveSync for a long time. It provides access to email, calendars, and contacts, but ActiveSync does not have all the features of a full-fledged MDM solution. ActiveSync allows smart devices to connect to the exchange server via the Internet. ActiveSync allows users to get access to many Outlook functionalities like email, calendars, contacts, and tasks.

ActiveSync also has the ability to enact policies that let an organization control sharing and remove access to the camera and other apps, but these policies depend on the platform, and popular devices, such as iOS and Android, are not supported. ActiveSync devices are administered by Microsoft Exchange. All connected devices can be inventoried after the device is connected to ActiveSync. ActiveSync, as mentioned earlier in this section, also allows to lock devices. Most importantly, ActiveSync can remotely wipe a smart device, to ensure that a lost or stolen phone will not contain stored corporate data.

The drawback of ActiveSync is that it cannot be used to set up access to other smart device resources. It is unable to push applications to devices, or configure VPN, Wi-fi, or other remote access. ActiveSync is limited when it comes to mobile device security on the more popular platforms. Also, it does not have the ability to control the security features of the device or detect jailbreaks.

11.5 Full MDM Solutions

There are large numbers of MDM solutions currently available, and new MDM vendors are surfacing every year. These solutions offer various benefits, from a *containerized, heavily fortified security approach* to *noncontainerized, user-flexible, and quickly implemented cloud-based solutions*. There is an MDM for almost every need, no matter the size of the business or the range of devices or operating systems. The following is a list of some of the most popular providers in the industry at present:

1. *AirWatch* comprises one of the most inclusive enterprise mobility management (EMM) solutions that scale across cloud and on-premises deployments. The platform supports containerization through its workspace feature, along with a *dual-persona* option that separates the personal and corporate resources on the devices. AirWatch was recently acquired by VMware and identified as a leader in the EMM space in Gartner's magic quadrant.

2. *MobileIron's EMM* is available as a cloud-based service or an on-premises platform and secures applications, content, and devices regardless of the device type, providing a native end-user experience. Leveraging MobileIron's application programming interfaces, organizations can integrate the platform with their existing IT infrastructure. MobileIron was also listed as a leader in Gartner's magic quadrant for enterprise mobility.

3. *Good Technology's enterprise mobility solution* focuses on application and content management, taking a less invasive approach to EMM than the other vendors. With the recent acquisition of BoxTone, Good Technology's MDM capabilities also include mobile service management, which offers a *single-pane-of-glass* visibility and management for IT administrators.

4. *IBM's MaaS360* acquired Fiberlink and has integrated the solution in its mobility management suite, offering an on-premises deployment option in addition to SaaS. IBM's MaaS360 was also ranked as a leader in EMM in Gartner's magic quadrant.

5. *Microsoft's Enterprise Mobility Suite* comprises the on-premises management capabilities of System Center Configuration Manager that are integrated with the cloud-based capabilities of Windows Intune, the Azure Active Directory for identity and access, and the Azure Rights Management Services for data protection.

6. *SAP Afaria* is the MDM portion of SAP's Mobile Secure portfolio that offers device, application, and content management, both in an on-premises and a cloud-based model. SAP Afaria was also the only challenger listed in Gartner's most recent magic quadrant for enterprise mobility.

7. *BlackBerry's BES10 EMM* suite is not limited to just BlackBerry devices. It offers support for Android, iOS, and, soon, Windows Phone 8 devices as well. BES10 is a cloud-based version of the service and is especially appealing to those organizations that continue to use BlackBerry within their enterprise.

8. *Citrix XenMobile* includes a suite of solutions that facilitate mobile device, application, and content management. Combining ShareFile, NetScaler, XenApp, and XenDesktop, the EMM solution is comprehensive. Citrix is working on integrating the various other administration consoles into a single-pane-of-glass experience.

9. *McAfee EMM* integrates its existing products to mobile devices, allowing IT to use the same platform and infrastructure to manage in-house and mobile devices from a single pane of glass. End users can take advantage of the self-service portal to provision and manage their own devices and receive alerts related to security or compliance issues.

10. *Amtel* is a cloud-based service that is able to deliver real-time device usage information for expense control and offers enterprise resource planning (ERP) integration, which is not a common enterprise mobility feature. It is worth noting that Amtel does not support Windows mobile devices at this time.

The top MDM solutions can support both corporate devices and personal BYOD smart devices. All MDM solutions are unique, and all have various levels of vendor support, integration into existing networks, different management capabilities, and user flexibility. Solutions can have a different approach to data security and user privacy. When making a decision on an MDM provider, it is important to look at integration and compatibility, capabilities and key features, management and usability, security and privacy, and, maybe, most importantly, the pricing.

12

REGISTERING SMART DEVICES

12.1 Introduction

Android, Apple iOS, Windows, and BlackBerry smart devices have support for mobile device management (MDM). MDM gives organizations the capability to manage smart devices throughout the company. MDM features vary from platform to platform and depend on the technologies that are built into the smartphone platform. Apple uses technologies such as Configuration Profiles and the Apple Push Notification service. Android uses the Android Device Administration application programming interface (API), built into Android 2.2 and higher devices. This gives information technology departments the ability to securely enroll smart devices in an enterprise environment and gives them the ability to configure and update settings, monitor compliance with corporate policies, and even remotely wipe or lock managed devices.

In the chapter, we will review the device enrollment specifications for the two most popular platforms, Android and Apple iOS, and describe how MDM can be used to register the smart devices. To illustrate how the MDM solution works, Microsoft's Intune* software is used throughout these chapters.

The following screenshots of device enrollment were performed on Microsoft Intune. Microsoft Intune is a cloud-based solution that provides MDM, mobile application management, and personal computer (PC) management capabilities.

For users to be able to enroll their mobile devices with Microsoft Intune, the system administrator must use a user account to interface

---

* The use of Microsoft's Intune does not imply that the authors are recommending this solution.

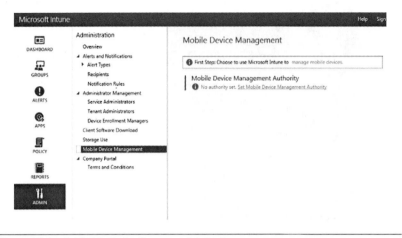

Figure 12.1 Set Mobile Device Management Authority.

with Intune. The user account can be an Office 365 account or an Active Directory account. First, declare Intune as the MDM authority. As Figure 12.1 shows, Microsoft Intune has been selected to perform MDM services.

The administrator can use an existing active directory account or an Office 365 account to sign in to the Intune management portal depending on configuration. Once logged in additional user accounts can be added and the Company Portal can be setup for users.

The next step in MDM is enabling the specific smart device platforms that are allowed in your environment. In this example, we will enable Apple iOS and Android management.

12.2 Enabling iOS Management

The administration of Apple iOS devices occurs by a connection to an MDM server. The iOS device connects with the MDM server and checks if there are any pending tasks and answers with the appropriate actions. The examples of tasks that can be performed are downloading or modifying policies, providing device information for reports, or changing configuration or removing data.

The MDM server communicates with an iOS device via a silent notification that is sent to the device through Apple's Push Notification (APN) Service. This causes the device to make a connection with the MDM server.

The organization's MDM server requires a certificate in order for the push notification server to recognize commands from it. This certificate must be requested and downloaded from the Apple Push Certificates Portal. We will illustrate this process using Microsoft Intune, as shown in Figure 12.2.

The first step in enabling iOS management for Intune or any MDM is to download a certificate signing request for an APN certificate (Figure 12.2). The downloaded certificate signing request (.csr) file is used to request a trust relationship certificate from the Apple Push Certificates Portal. After downloading the file, the next step is to go to the Apple Push Certificates Portal and sign in with a company Apple ID to create the APN certificate using the .csr file (Figure 12.3). Once the file is created, you must then download the certificate (.pem) file.

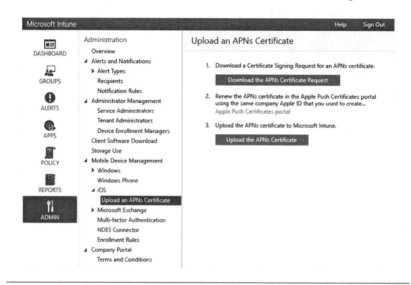

Figure 12.2   Microsoft Intune: Upload an APN Certificate Menu.

Figure 12.3   Apple Push Certificates Portal.

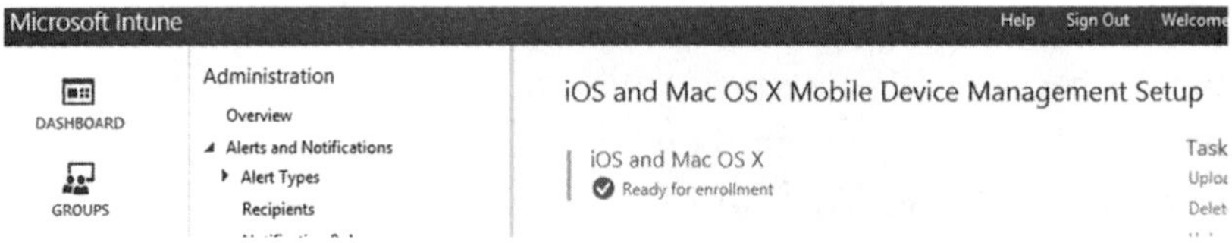

Figure 12.4 Microsoft Intune: iOS setup completed confirmation.

Next, from the Intune console (Figure 12.4), upload the APN Certificate, and now the Intune MDM tool can enroll and manage iOS devices.

12.3 Enabling Android

Android does not have a comparable process, as there is no push notification service needed to manage Android devices. Android 2.2 and above utilize the Android Device Administration API. The Device Administration API provides device administration features at the system level. In Android, an administration application is installed on the device, and it enforces security policies. These policies could be built into the app or could be retrieved from an MDM server. When users install and enable the device admin application, they agree to accept its policies, benefits, and administration. In Intune, no additional configurations in the Intune console are needed to enable Android mobile device enrollment.

12.3.1 Device Enrollment

After the MDM server has been configured to the correct specifications, the next step is to enroll the device with the MDM server. Device enrollment establishes the relationship between the device and the server, allowing it to be managed by the server. Registration options vary depending on the platform. On Android, device registration occurs through the installation of a mobile app. On Apple iOS, this can be done by connecting the iPhone or the iPad to a computer via a Universal Serial Bus, but most solutions deliver the enrollment profile wirelessly. Most MDM solutions use a mobile app to guide users to this process; others initiate enrollment by directing users to a Web portal.

There are multiple ways that the MDM installation application can be installed on users' devices. Some of the ways an organization may distribute the application to the users are an official app store (Google Play or Apple App Store), or another app store (that may be established for the organization), through email or Websites.

In this example for Microsoft Intune, we will start with downloading the Intune app via the Google Play and Apple app stores.

Android Enrollment via Google Play

> *Step 1:* The user must search the Google Play Store for the *Intune Company Portal* app (Figure 12.5).
>
> *Step 2:* Once located, the user must download and install the Intune Company Portal app (Figure 12.6). The user must accept the permissions that the app requests.
>
> *Step 3:* Once the app is installed, the user must open the app and authenticate against his or her Office 365 or an Active Directory account (Figure 12.7).

Figure 12.5   Locating the Intune Company Portal app on an Android device in Google Play.

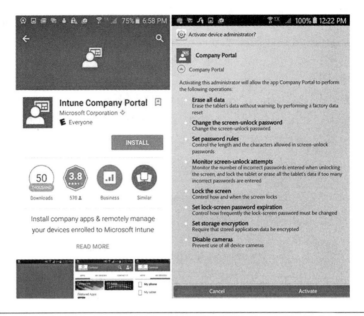

Figure 12.6 The Intune Company Portal app in the Google Play store and the Review permissions screens.

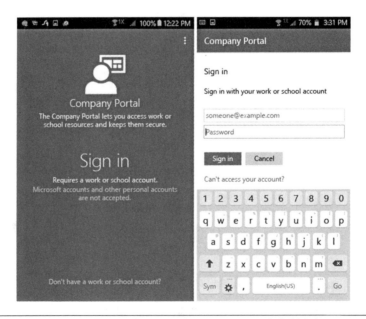

Figure 12.7 The Intune Company Portal app sign in screens on an Android device.

Step 4: After authentication, the Intune portal app presents the user with screens describing what the administrator can access on his or her device (Figure 12.8).

Figure 12.8 The Intune Company Portal app provides guidance and information to users during setup on an Android device.

iOS Enrollment via the Apple App Store

Step 1: The user must search the Apple App Store for the Intune Company Portal App (Figure 12.9). Once located, the user must download and install the Intune Company Portal App.

Figure 12.9 Locating the Intune Company Portal app on an iOS device in Apple's App Store.

Figure 12.10 The Intune Company Portal app sign in screens on an iOS device.

Step 2: Once the app is installed, the user must open the app and authenticate using their Office 365 or Active Directory credentials (Figure 12.10).

Step 3: After authentication, the Intune portal app presents the user with screens describing what the administrator can access on his or her device (Figure 12.11).

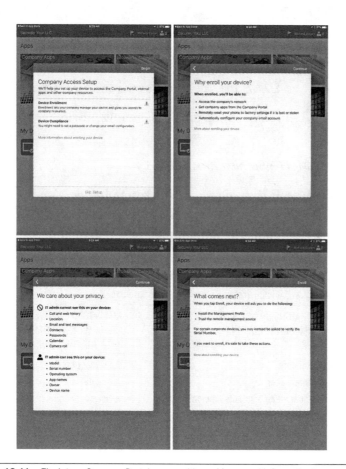

Figure 12.11   The Intune Company Portal app provides guidance and information to users during setup on an iOS device.

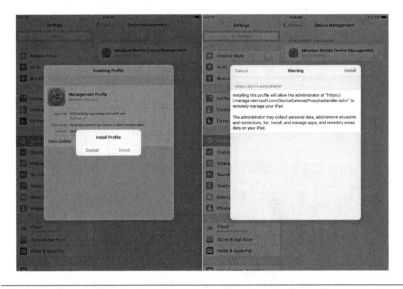

Figure 12.12 The Intune Company Portal app installing a configuration profile on an iOS device.

Step 4: The users must install and accept the

configuration profile (Figure 12.12).

12.3.2 MDM Administrator Access Authority

Users who enroll their device in Microsoft Intune give the MDM administrator the permission to manage their smart device. Table 12.1 shows a description of what administrators have and do not have access to.

Table 12.1 Administrators Authority in MDM Software

ADMINISTRATORS DO NOT HAVE ACCESS TO INFORMATION PERTAINING TO THE FOLLOWING:	ADMINISTRATORS DO HAVE ACCESS TO INFORMATION PERTAINING TO THE FOLLOWING:
• Call history	• The owner of the device
• Text messages	• Device name
• Personal email, contacts, and calendar	• Device serial number
• Web history	• Device manufacturer
• Location	• Device model
• Camera roll	• Device OS
• Personal data	• Company apps installed
	• Personal apps installed

12.3.3 MDM Administrator Authority

The MDM administrator has the following abilities on Android and Apple iOS devices (Table 12.2).

MDM device enrollment can be a deal-breaker. If a solution cannot effectively enroll users, it could be a disaster. Most MDM solutions

Table 12.2 Microsoft Intune Capabilities on iOS and Android

MICROSOFT MDM ABILITIES ON ANDROID	MICROSOFT MDM ABILITIES ON APPLE iOS
• Reset your device back to manufacturer's defaults. This is helpful if the device is lost or stolen.	• Reset your device back to manufacturer's default settings if the device is lost or stolen.
• Remove all company-related data. Your personal data and settings aren't removed.	• Remove all installed, company-related data and business apps. Your personal data and settings aren't removed.
• Force you to have a password or PIN on the device, which may lock you out of the device, or reset your device back to manufacturer's default settings, which may include the deletion of data, if there are too many incorrect password attempts.	• Require you to have a password or PIN on the device.
• Require you to accept terms and conditions.	• Require you to accept terms and conditions.
• Enable or disable the camera on your device.	• Enable or disable the camera on your device.
• Force all the data, including corporate and personal data, on the device to be encrypted. This helps protect the data if the device is lost or stolen.	• Enable or disable Web browsing on your device.
• After your device is added to the Company Portal, approximately every 8 hours, it will do the following:	• Enable or disable backup to iCloud.
• Download any policy or app updates that your IT administrator has made available.	• Enable or disable document sync to iCloud.
• Send any hardware inventory updates. (These updates do not contain personal information.)	• Enable or disable Photo Stream to iCloud.
• Send any company app inventory updates. (These updates do not contain personal information.)	• Enable or disable data roaming on your device. If data roaming is allowed, roaming charges may be incurred.
	• Enable or disable voice roaming on your device. If voice roaming is allowed, roaming charges may be incurred.
	• Enable or disable automatic file synchronization while in roaming mode on your device. If automatic file synchronization is allowed, roaming charges may be incurred.

have similar enrollment features to Microsoft Intune, but there could be a number of differences. There are a constantly increasing number of MDM solution choices available to organizations; research should be done to determine how your perspective solution handles device enrollment.

13

PROVISIONING EMAIL, CALENDAR, AND CONTACTS

13.1 Introduction

Email has undoubtedly become one of the major forms of communication in the business world. On a single day, millions of emails are received and delivered from organizations to customers and partners, from staff members to their managers, and between coworkers. Email communication has many benefits; it is sent and received almost instantaneously; it is a great tool for record keeping; it is one of the most cost-efficient methods of communication; and it is an excellent marketing tool. Given how much email is used every day, it is hard to imagine how business ever functioned without it.

Smart devices have greatly benefited from the mass use of email as a business communication tool. Email is one the most used features of smart devices. Smart device email use is not limited to business, but it is also now common for personal use. The current smart devices have built-in email client support for both corporate and personal email. Popular email services such as Windows Live Mail, Gmail, and Yahoo are all easily accessible right out of the box.

Corporate email is mostly handled through a corporate email server like Microsoft Exchange, Novell GroupWise, or Lotus Notes. Many smart devices support Internet Message Access Protocol or Post Office Protocol configuration to receive email, but these protocols do not offer the security features that many organizations require such as remote wipe abilities. One of the most common methods for secure email and calendar syncing from corporate email servers is Exchange ActiveSync.

13.2 Email Access Using ActiveSync

Microsoft Exchange ActiveSync is a communication protocol, based on Hypertext Transfer Protocol and Extensible Markup Language, that pushes email, calendar, contacts, and *to-do* items on your smart devices from a corporate email server (Figure 13.1). The device user has the ability to continue to access this information on their device, even when they are offline and not connected to ActiveSync. Any changes made by the user on the device related to email, calendar, contacts and to-do items are sent to the corporate server when the device connects to ActiveSync. The ActiveSync connection can be made directly from the device using Wi-fi or a cellular network. ActiveSync facilitates the process of reconciling data to the corresponding device and the correct mailbox. ActiveSync is a popular solution for smart device email, calendar, and contact device synchronization for many companies.

Most of the popular smart devices currently on the market support ActiveSync, including Android, BlackBerry, Apple iOS, and Windows Phones.

Apple iOS devices are compatible with Exchange and can use the device's native email and calendar applications. The Account Wizard supports Microsoft Exchange and is easy to set up with the required account information. With ActiveSync, contacts and

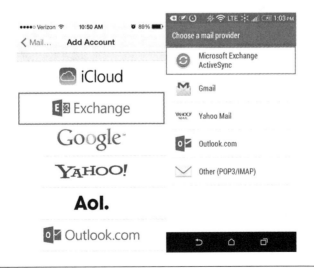

Figure 13.1 Microsoft ActiveSync setup screen.

calendar information can be synched with the native Calendar app. Usually, there is no need for any special application to be installed.

Android smart devices also have native support for Microsoft ActiveSync. After entering the required information for configuration, all email, contacts, and calendar information can be synched with the native email client, contact, and calendar applications. Usually, there is no need for any special application to be installed.

Exchange email server users have Exchange ActiveSync device access enabled by default. Administrators must disable it if employees are not allowed to connect their compatible devices. Administrators have the option of granting access to all employees, but they can also restrict access to parties that do not require device access to Exchange. Exchange ActiveSync can be configured to use Secure Sockets Layer encryption for communications between the Exchange server and the smart device.

Authentication can be performed using a self-signed certificate, a certificate from an existing public key infrastructure, or a third-party commercial certificate. Exchange ActiveSync can use certificate-based authentication together with other security features. It has support for RSA Secure-ID two-factor authentication on the Exchange server. Exchange ActiveSync has an Autodiscover feature that allows a user to set up their mobile device to receive email simply by entering their email address and password. This allows for easy setup for administrators while offering a great set of robust features.

13.3 Email Security Options within ActiveSync

Administrators have several options in maintaining security in their email environments. Exchange ActiveSync has a feature called mailbox policies. These policies can be applied to the users in the corporate environment. The policy feature gives administrators control over the functionality of connected devices. The administrator has an option of either applying a policy to a given user or not having to apply a policy to a user. By default, users are allowed to sync their devices without any restrictions and do not have a password policy requirement. Conveniently, the default policy allows devices to be remotely wiped. The remote wipe feature is great for lost or stolen devices. A remote wipe restores the device to factory condition but does not erase the previously downloaded system updates. A remote wipe may differ from platform to platform. Users can initiate a remote wipe themselves, or it can be performed by an administrator. When a remote wipe is issued, a command is sent to the device; when received, the wipe occurs the next time the device attempts to sync to the corporate server. A device that that runs out of power, or does not have a connection, will not perform the wipe because it has not received the command.

Assigning policies for users can be difficult because every device may not support every policy setting. Mailbox policies allow administrators to configure the features and security settings to apply to users. Table 13.1, provided by Microsoft TechNet, summarizes the settings that you can specify using mobile device mailbox policies.

Unless an organization has some other mobile device management solution, Microsoft ActiveSync is an important way to maintain the security of smart devices that are connected to the email server. Microsoft Exchange ActiveSync supports the majority of device platforms, including Apple iOS, Windows, Android, and BlackBerry, without the need for additional applications. Exchange ActiveSync allows the smart devices used for email to require the ability to remotely wipe a device and enforce password requirements; this should be a minimum security baseline for organizations.

Table 13.1 ActiveSync Mobile Device Mailbox Policy Options

SETTING	DESCRIPTION
Allow Bluetooth	This setting specifies whether a mobile device allows Bluetooth connections. The available options are Disable, HandsFree Only, and Allow. The default value is Allow. The Exchange Enterprise Client Access License is required to change the values of this setting.
Allow browser	This setting specifies whether Pocket Internet Explorer is allowed on the mobile device. This setting does not affect third-party browsers installed on the mobile device. The default value is $true. The Exchange Enterprise Client Access License is required to change the values of this setting.
Allow camera	This setting specifies whether the mobile device camera can be used. The default value is $true. The Exchange Enterprise Client Access License is required to change the values of this setting.
Allow consumer email	This setting specifies whether the mobile device user can configure a personal email account (either POP3 or IMAP4) on the mobile device. The default value is $true. This setting does not control access to email accounts that are using third-party mobile device email programs. The Exchange Enterprise Client Access License is required to change the values of this setting.
Allow desktop sync	This setting specifies whether the mobile device can synchronize with a computer through a cable, Bluetooth, or IrDA connection. The default value is $true. The Exchange Enterprise Client Access License is required to change the values of this setting.
Allow external device management	This setting specifies whether an external device management program is allowed to manage the mobile device.
Allow HTML email	This setting specifies whether the email synchronized to the mobile device can be in HTML format. If this setting is set to $false, all email is converted to plain text.
Allow internet sharing	This setting specifies whether the mobile device can be used as a modem for a desktop or a portable computer. The default value is $true. The Exchange Enterprise Client Access License is required to change the values of this setting.
Allow IrDA	This setting specifies whether infrared connections are allowed to and from the mobile device. The Exchange Enterprise Client Access License is required to change the values of this setting.

(*Continued*)

Table 13.1 (Continued)   ActiveSync Mobile Device Mailbox Policy Options

SETTING	DESCRIPTION
Allow mobile OTA update	This setting specifies whether the mobile device mailbox policy settings can be sent to the mobile device over a cellular data connection. The default value is $true.
Allow non-provisionable devices	This setting specifies whether mobile devices that may not support application of all policy settings are allowed to connect to Exchange 2013 by using Exchange ActiveSync. Allowing nonprovisionable mobile devices has security implications. For example, some nonprovisionable devices may not be able to implement an organization's password requirements.
Allow POP/IMAP email	This setting specifies whether the user can configure a POP3 or an IMAP4 email account on the mobile device. The default value is $true. This setting does not control access by third-party email programs.
Allow remote desktop	This setting specifies whether the mobile device can initiate a remote desktop connection. The default value is $true. The Exchange Enterprise Client Access License is required to change the values of this setting.
Allow simple password	This setting enables or disables the ability to use a simple password such as 1111 or 1234. The default value is $true.
Allow S/MIME encryption algorithm negotiation	This setting specifies whether the messaging application on the mobile device can negotiate the encryption algorithm if a recipient's certificate does not support the specified encryption algorithm.
Allow S/MIME software certificates	This setting specifies whether S/MIME software certificates are allowed on the mobile device.
Allow storage card	This setting specifies whether the mobile device can access information that is stored on a storage card. The Exchange Enterprise Client Access License is required to change the values of this setting.
Allow text messaging	This setting specifies whether text messaging is allowed from the mobile device. The default value is $true. The Exchange Enterprise Client Access License is required to change the values of this setting.
Allow unsigned applications	This setting specifies whether unsigned applications can be installed on the mobile device. The default value is $true. The Exchange Enterprise Client Access License is required to change the values of this setting.
Allow unsigned installation packages	This setting specifies whether an unsigned installation package can be run on the mobile device. The default value is $true. The Exchange Enterprise Client Access License is required to change the values of this setting.

(Continued)

Table 13.1 (Continued)   ActiveSync Mobile Device Mailbox Policy Options

SETTING	DESCRIPTION
Allow Wi-fi	This setting specifies whether wireless Internet access is allowed on the mobile device. The default value is $\mathtt{\$true}$. The Exchange Enterprise Client Access License is required to change the values of this setting.
Alphanumeric password required	This setting requires that a password contains numeric and non-numeric characters. The default value is $\mathtt{\$true}$.
Approved application list	This setting stores a list of approved applications that can be run on the mobile device. The Exchange Enterprise Client Access License is required to change the values of this setting.
Attachments enabled	This setting enables attachments to be downloaded to the mobile device. The default value is $\mathtt{\$true}$.
Device encryption enabled	This setting enables encryption on the mobile device. Not all mobile devices can enforce encryption. For more information, see the device and mobile OS documentation.
Device policy refresh interval	This setting specifies how often the mobile device mailbox policy is sent from the server to the mobile device.
IRM enabled	This setting specifies whether Information Rights Management (IRM) is enabled on the mobile device.
Max attachment size	This setting controls the maximum size of attachments that can be downloaded to the mobile device. The default value is Unlimited.
Max calendar age filter	This setting specifies the maximum range of calendar days that can be synchronized to the mobile device. The following values are accepted: 1. All 2. OneDay 3. ThreeDays 4. OneWeek 5. TwoWeeks 6. OneMonth
Max email age filter	This setting specifies the maximum number of days of email items to synchronize to the mobile device. The following values are accepted: 1. All 2. OneDay 3. ThreeDays 4. OneWeek 5. TwoWeeks 6. OneMonth
Max email body truncation size	This setting specifies the maximum size at which email messages are truncated when synchronized to the mobile device. The value is in kilobytes (KB).

(Continued)

Table 13.1 (Continued) ActiveSync Mobile Device Mailbox Policy Options

SETTING	DESCRIPTION
Max email HTML body truncation size	This setting specifies the maximum size at which Hypertext Markup Language (HTML) email messages are truncated when synchronized to the mobile device. The value is in kilobytes (KB).
Max inactivity time lock	This value specifies the length of time that the mobile device can be inactive before a password is required to reactivate it. You can enter any interval between 30 seconds and 1 hour. The default value is 15 minutes.
Max password failed attempts	This setting specifies the number of attempts a user can make to enter the correct password for the mobile device. You can enter any number from 4 to 16. The default value is 8.
Min password complex characters	This setting specifies the minimum number of complex characters required in the mobile device's password. A complex character is a character that is not a letter.
Min password length	This setting specifies the minimum number of characters in the mobile device password. You can enter any number from 1 to 16. The default value is 4.
Password enabled	This setting enables the mobile device password.
Password expiration	This setting enables the administrator to configure a length of time after which a mobile device password must be changed.
Password history	This setting specifies the number of past passwords that can be stored in a user's mailbox. A user cannot reuse a stored password.
Password recovery enabled	When this setting is enabled, the mobile device generates a recovery password that is sent to the server. If the user forgets their mobile device password, the recovery password can be used to unlock the mobile device and enable the user to create a new mobile device password.
Require device encryption	This setting specifies whether device encryption is required. If set to $true, the mobile device must be able to support and implement encryption to synchronize with the server.
Require encrypted S/MIME messages	This setting specifies whether S/MIME messages must be encrypted. The default value is $false.
Require encryption S/MIME algorithm	This setting specifies what required algorithm must be used when encrypting S/MIME messages.
Require manual synchronization while roaming	This setting specifies whether the mobile device must synchronize manually while roaming. Allowing automatic synchronization while roaming will frequently lead to larger-than-expected data costs for the mobile device data plan.
Require signed S/MIME algorithm	This setting specifies what required algorithm must be used when signing a message.

(*Continued*)

Table 13.1 (Continued)   ActiveSync Mobile Device Mailbox Policy Options

SETTING	DESCRIPTION
Require signed S/MIME messages	This setting specifies whether the mobile device must send signed S/MIME messages.
Require storage card encryption	This setting specifies whether the storage card must be encrypted. Not all mobile device OSs support storage card encryption. For more information, see your mobile device and mobile OS documentation.
Unapproved InROM application list	This setting specifies a list of applications that cannot be run in read-only memory. The Exchange Enterprise Client Access License is required to change the values of this setting.

14

APPLICATION DEVELOPMENT AND DEPLOYMENT

14.1 Introduction

It is beneficial for organizations to take advantage of deploying an effective smart device development strategy. Currently, users are spending more and more time on their phone or other smart devices. In this current climate, it is essential that organizations have a presence via a *smart device–friendly* Website or a smart device app. A smart device app or a Web app can create opportunities for improvement in employee productivity and better engagement with customers. Organizations can leverage this opportunity by creating applications that align with their overall business strategy.

In this chapter, we will give you an overall understanding of smart device application development and discuss some of the decisions that must be made when deciding to develop a smart device application.

14.2 Smart Device App Considerations

The first step in enterprise smart device application development is determining what apps your employees and customers are currently using and if a new application with a different functionality would be advantageous for your business. Custom-made applications can improve productivity and greatly increase customer engagement and provide organizations with a competitive advantage. Once organizations have an app idea, they should decide if the idea aligns with your goals and objectives. This is extremely important when determining the value of the smart device app idea that you wish to develop.

If the determination is to actually move forward with this app, you must ask and answer the following questions before you can start the development process:

- Who is your target audience, and what needs do they have?
- What are the best ways to reach the audience?
- What will motivate them to use this app?
- What characteristics does our app need to successfully satisfy the customer's expectations?

There are many types of apps with a varied target audience. Apps can be external facing for customers, vendors, employees, etc. Apps can also be internal facing for sales department, human resources, etc. The design of your application must keep this goal in mind: *to design and develop a mobile app that is best suited for its audience.*

The development of a smart device application is only a part of the overall project. The other half is the management of the app. The management of applications includes activities such as testing, distribution, and application support. Mobile operating systems are constantly changing and evolving. These changes can cause your app to malfunction because of an operating system change. It is important that your applications are prepared for this eventual change. Managing the application is just as important as developing it.

Most enterprise smart device apps are not stand alone. Some applications require infrastructure components that need to be obtained, in order to create your smart device app. Organizations must put a lot of planning into designing the necessary infrastructure requirements for their smart device project. These infrastructure needs may include the need for managing security across various devices and app distribution methods such as an MDM solution or an app store. Also needed is the creation of environments to test the app through its various development phases, before moving the app into production. A determination must be made to select the correct vendors to partner with and to provide the necessary infrastructure components that fit your application's vision. Is there a way to leverage open source technologies in order to save money?

Development from scratch may not be the best way for your organization to create your desired smart device app. There are over a million apps on Android and Apple iOS. If a similar solution to your application idea already exists, *why reinvent the wheel?* When deciding to get into application development, it is best to do your due diligence. Determine if purchasing an off-the-shelf application would be more beneficial than developing applications from scratch. Smart device application development is a long, expensive, and difficult process. Why go through that process if another solution could fit your needs with a bit of customization? Compare the cost of developing a mobile app from scratch as opposed to purchasing an off-the-shelf solution. Measure the length of development time in purchasing versus creating your applications. All of these topics should be considered before a smart device app development project is initiated.

Identifying the best smart device development strategy for your organization should start with deciding the right approach. Should you choose a smart device app, a smart device Website, a fully responsive Website, or a combination approach? There are benefits and drawbacks to each of these approaches. In order to make an informed decision, it is important to have a good understanding of what each entails.

14.3 Smart Device Applications

Smart device apps are downloaded and installed on the smart device itself. These apps usually come from the platform's designated app store (such as the Apple App Store and Google Play). But they could also be distributed via a mobile device management (MDM) solution or a company-designated app store. The platform's designated app store contain apps specifically designed for devices running that operating system. Smart device apps can retrieve content from the Internet similar to a Website. Smart device apps can implement platform-specific features that mobile Websites do not have the ability to perform. An app can leverage the hardware capabilities of smart devices far greater than mobile Websites; features such as the accelerometer (measures and monitors the movement of a device), a built-in Global Positioning System, the microphone, and native platform application programming interfaces have more functionality.

Smart device apps also have the ability to maintain functionality in the absence of an Internet connection. While running an app, users can still access application content even if their device is not within the range of cellular service. Lots of people think of smart device apps mainly for the purpose of casual gaming, but apps have many functionalities that can improve the user's productivity. One of the greatest advantages that apps have over Websites is the ability to store data locally on the device. Another advantage is that the smart devices generally offer more advanced encryption options compared to most Websites.

There are some advantages to mobile Websites over smart device apps. Apps require users to initially download and install the app; this is an additional step for them. Apps often require upgrades; when this happens, users will be required to perform additional downloads. The users of a mobile Website do not have this problem. Apps must also be developed for each platform, unlike mobile Websites that should function on any device with a browser. Smart device apps are usually more expensive to develop and maintain. They also tend to be more time consuming on the development side. If you are operating on a limited budget, and you want to target multiple devices, a mobile Website may be a better option for your organization.

14.4 Smart Device Website

There is a good chance that your organization has a Website. But can your site be accessed and function properly on a smart device? Most Websites are simply not smart device friendly. A lot of Websites were designed with computers in mind and have not been revamped in the smart device age. Smart device users often visit pages that have huge loading times, buttons that are too small to click, flash animation that is incompatible, and/or graphics that are not scaled properly for their device. A smart device Website is the answer to most of these problems as it is designed specifically for smart device displays and touch screens.

A lot of Websites detect the device and forward users to the proper version of their site (such as a www.website.com being redirected to an *m.website.com* address). In this scenario, the Website should have a version of their site for phones, tablets, and any other device that you wish to support.

This works great if your primary goal is to deliver simple content to smart devices or perform a service that does not have requirements to save data or access device hardware features. Restaurant finder Websites, such as Yelp, offer a mobile Website in addition to their Website, and the site mimics app experience. Smart device Websites are usually a limited version of the standard Website. They are mostly used for simple actions and provide important details or functions.

A fully responsive design is a flexible site that seamlessly transitions between the Web, tablet, and mobile devices, usually without losing content. Sites like these use a Web technology called *media query*. Media query allows Web developers to specify a particular type of screen and/or certain device conditions such as device width, height, or orientation. Based on the response from the media query, the Website can specify how the Web content will appear on that device. When viewing a responsive site on a computer or a laptop, the content may appear in two columns. With the same site on a smaller display, such as a phone or a tablet, that same content may condense into a single column. A responsive Website will even transform the images, buttons, and text and resize them as the user expands or reduces the browser window.

Responsive sites are good for mirror content on multiple devices. Unlike mobile sites and apps that often provide limited or condensed content, a fully responsive site should maintain the entirety of your content and provide it in an optimized format depending on the user's device. But, for a specific smart device user, it may be preferable to have a small snapshot of information delivered on a phone, instead of large amounts of possibly overwhelming information. For instance, a phone user may only wish to see your service and not want to read about your organization's entire history.

With so many different devices used by potential smart device users, a fully responsive site seems like an essential solution, even if you decide to develop an app. A fully responsive site takes a great deal of development time, but it makes perfect sense to design one Website that can be fully optimized across many different types of smart devices.

Usually, the most desired and best functioning experience for users is through the smart device app. Apps are, by far, the most difficult way to make your presence felt on a smart device, but, when done right, it is a thing of beauty.

14.5 Application Development

Smart device applications are transforming the way we communicate, do business, and consume news and entertainment. Businesses and consumers have embraced this innovative technology, thus making mobile applications a highly demanded service. The increase in smart device users has caused tremendous growth in the rise in the number of smart device application platforms. There is great deal of diversity in the chosen platform; many select one of the two most popular smart device operating systems currently available: Apple's iOS and Android.

The Android application development mainly uses Java code. Java is a common programming language that is used by developers. This makes finding developers for Android much easier for most organizations. Apple's iOS uses Apple's Objective-C language, which is similar to developers who already have experience with C and C++. With Objective-C being a newer language, it is often harder to find experienced programmers.

Android, being a more open platform, allows developers the choice to use a great deal of third-party tools for app development. This also provides an easier way to add more features and functionalities. This helps the growth of the platform and improves Android development in general. Conversely, Apple iOS development is, by far, more restrictive in their developer guidelines. In iOS development, the developer is forced to use a fixed set of tools in which to develop. This makes iOS far more difficult and limits creativity.

14.6 Application Distribution

The barriers to distribution also differ on both platforms. On the Apple App Store, it takes one to two weeks for an app to get approval. Apple places many restrictions on the apps that can be distributed from their app store. The Google Play Store presents no approval process for the developer. An application can be submitted and available for distribution in less than 24 hours, which also makes the update to the applications far more convenient for an Android developer.

No matter which platform(s) you choose, if done correctly, the end result should be the same. The ultimate goal of this process is to develop an effective smart device application that should enable your targeted audience to perform a specific set of related tasks. Developing smart device apps for your organizational needs is a major way to improve your productivity and/or customer engagement. There is a tremendous amount to decide when taking the development avenue, and proper planning is of utmost importance. Smart device development can be time consuming and expensive, but, if done correctly, the benefits can greatly outweigh the cost.

15

CONNECTING TO CORPORATE NETWORK

15.1 Introduction

The use of smart devices in the corporate environment has experienced tremendous growth in this decade. These devices can be a great business tool for an organization; they allow users to instantly access information, conduct research, and communicate with others, increasing the speed of productivity. Smart devices are just as common as desktops or laptops for Internet access. It is extremely likely that employees will have their own smart device and bring it to your environment every day. The burden will be placed on the organization's information technology (IT) department to provide technical support and thought leadership on proper usage. This creates huge problems for the organization; smart devices can expose a corporate network to a larger number of new threats.

Smart devices move in and out of the network, passing through internal and external firewalls. The smart devices in your network could be bring your own device (BYOD), corporate issued, personally enabled or company owned. It is more difficult for the corporate IT department to control what actions the users are taking with a smart device; as a result, it can expose an organization to new security threats. In this chapter, we will discuss the technical network capabilities of popular smart device platforms and provide insight on the issues with connecting these devices to the corporate network.

15.2 Dangers of Smart Devices to the Corporate Network

The dangers of smart devices to the corporate network are many. Unsafe employee device use can increase the potential for data loss or data leakage. This can be caused by lost/stolen devices, unauthorized device access, and unauthorized or unintended data transmission. Strong security is important when dealing with smart devices on the network. Authentication and authorization must be strongly enforced to maintain secure network access. Employees' smart devices can contain critical information vital to the security of your network; at the same time, these devices are more susceptible to loss or theft. They can possibly contain network access keys, account information, and passwords. Smart devices are also vulnerable to many of the same dangers that face traditional computer operating systems (OSs). These devices can spread malware infections that come from email spam or phishing attempts and allow them to disseminate into your network.

Organizations also have the added problem of trying to support an ever-growing number of smart device platforms with different OS versions. In a personal computing environment, IT has the capability to ensure that computers have the latest patches and security updates installed, but, in the diverse landscape of smart devices, this becomes far more challenging. Organizations should consider all smart devices as uncontrolled endpoints and strongly consider establishing proper security controls. Technologies such as Secure Sockets Layer, virtual private networks (VPNs), and next-generation firewalls with application intelligence and control will help maintain the stability and security of the network.

15.3 Connecting a Smart Device to a VPN

A virtual private network is a term that describes a network that is constructed by using public access, most often via the Internet, to establish a connection to a private network, such as an organization or other private networks. A VPN transmits network data to the connected device by using the Internet for transportation. In order to maintain security, a VPN uses encryption and other security mechanisms to ensure that only authenticated parties can gain access to the VPN and ensures that the data cannot be compromised.

Organizations often use a VPN connection to communicate privately over a public data network. A VPN is an excellent option for smart devices as it is often more portable. VPN connections allow smart devices to share data in a confidential manner. An early problem that many organizations experienced when trying to support new smart device platforms was that the VPN technology support for industry standard protocols was limited. But, at present, the VPN technology for many smart device platforms has greatly improved. Let us review the two most popular types of smart device platform support for VPN technologies.

15.4 Apple iOS VPN Support

Apple iOS devices can use the following protocols and authentication methods (Figure 15.1):

- L2TP/IPSec with user authentication by MS-CHAP v2 Password, RSA SecurID, or CRYPTOCard, and machine authentication by shared secret.
- Point to Point Tunneling Protocol (PPTP) with user authentication by MS-CHAP v2 Password, RSA SecurID, or CRYPTOCard.

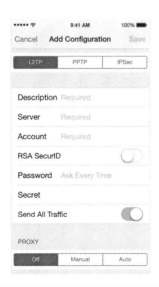

Figure 15.1 VPN configuration for Apple iOS.

- Cisco IPSec with user authentication by Password, RSA SecurID, or CRYPTOCard, and machine authentication by shared secret and certificates. Cisco IPSec works with VPN on Demand with the domains that you specify.
- Devices can also use third-party VPN apps available on the App Store. These apps might use other protocols.

15.5 Android VPN Support

- *PPTP:* User authentication by MS-CHAP v2 password, certificate, and two-factor token.
- *L2TP over IPSec:* User authentication by MS-CHAP v2 password, two-factor token, certificate, and machine authentication by shared secret or certificate.
- *Cisco IPSec:* User authentication by password, two-factor token, and machine authentication by shared secret and certificates.
- Devices can also use third-party VPN apps. These apps might use other protocols. Figures 15.1 through 15.3 show how VPN can be configured on an Apple iOS device.

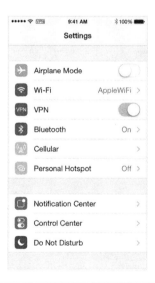

Figure 15.2 Turning VPN on in Apple iOS.

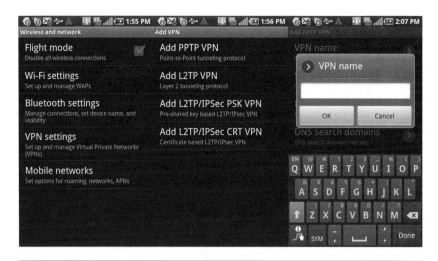

Figure 15.3 Adding VPN in Apple iOS.

15.6 Types of VPN Available to Smart Devices

15.6.1 Always-On VPN

Always-on VPN is a type of VPN that maintains a constant connection for device traffic by tunneling all Internet Protocol (IP) traffic back to the VPN network. It provides secures traffic transmission with data encryption. The network can now monitor and filter the smart device's network traffic and secure data transmission within the network, and it prevents direct device access to the Internet. For iOS devices, an always-on VPN activation requires that the device be in supervision mode. When the always-on VPN is activated on a smart device, the VPN automatically activates when an Internet connection is made. The VPN connection is maintained until the always-on VPN setting is turned off, or the device loses Internet connection. An always-on-VPN–connected device's VPN tunnel is tied to the Internet connection state. When the device interface gains an IP address, it tries to create a secure VPN tunnel. When the interface IP state goes down, the tunnel is terminated.

The always-on VPN on smart devices will create multiple tunnels for each network interface. For instance, Apple iOS devices create one VPN tunnel for the cellular interface and one VPN tunnel for the Wi-fi connection if both network interfaces are activated. All traffic from both interfaces moves through these VPN tunnels. This includes all Internet browsers, email, and other application traffic. Since all traffic moves through your VPN server, an organization can get a full view of the employees' Internet usage and block any distracting, inappropriate, or dangerous content.

15.6.2 Per-User/Per-Profile VPN

Most smart devices are designed for a single user, but Android version 4.2 introduced multi-user support (Figure 15.4). An Android device can be configured to allow multiple users, each of whom maintains their own separate home screen setup, apps, wallpaper, and general settings. As of now, Apple iOS devices only support a single user. If multiple users wanted to share an Apple VPN-connected device, they would have to share the VPN connection. This is not the case for Android; it supports per-user VPN on multiuser devices. On a per-user VPN, a tunnel is applied to each user to allow a user to route all network traffic through a VPN without affecting other users on the device.

Android 5.0 and above instituted managed profiles. This allows organizations to create configurations that isolate corporate data from personal data. An Android profile is similar to a user account, but it is tied to the primary user so that certain items are shared such as notifications and the recent task list. The Android work profile user maintains a strong separation between business and personal profiles. In this situation, Android also supports per-profile VPN. This VPN is applied per work profile, which allows an IT administrator to make sure that

Figure 15.4 Android introduces multi-user support.

only enterprise-designated network traffic goes through the organization's work profile VPN. In this situation, personal traffic would be excluded from the VPN.

15.6.3 Per-App VPN

Android and Apple iOS VPN connections can be set up on a per-app basis. This provides greater control over what kind of data goes through a VPN connection. On a normal VPN, all traffic, no matter how insignificant, routes through the VPN tunnel. The per-app VPN creates the ability to separate network traffic by the individual app. This assists administrators in separating personal from organizational data. This feature is most effective in a BYOD environment. The per-app VPN provides secure networking for traffic on internal corporate apps while also allowing users to keep personal network traffic separate.

Per-app VPN is managed by a mobile device management solution that designates what VPN each app is configured to use and excludes the unmanaged apps from using the VPN. Also, managed apps can be set up using different VPN connections. In this scenario, a human resources department app could use a different VPN from the IT department's app.

15.6.4 VPN on Demand

Apple also has a technology called *VPN on Demand*. This allows Apple iOS devices to automatically establish a VPN connection when needed. VPN on Demand uses a certificate-based authentication and works with various VPN protocols. This is configured using the *On Demand Rules key* in the VPN payload of a configuration profile. The rules can be defined into two properties:

1. *Network detection stage:* This defines the VPN requirements that are applied when the device's primary network connection changes.
2. *Connection evaluation stage:* This defines the VPN requirements for connection requests to domain names on an as-needed basis.

The VPN on Demand Rules can do the following:

- Determine if an Apple iOS device is connected to an internal network, and a VPN is not required
- Determine if an unknown Wi-fi network is being used and require a VPN connection for all network activities
- Mandate that a VPN connection be established when a Domain Name System request for a specified domain name fails

15.7 Importance of VPN to Smart Device Usage

A VPN provides secure access to an organization's private networks. VPN connections keep a user's communications secure and encrypted and away from prying eyes. Most mature smart device platforms have support for popular industry-standard VPN protocols by default. If your organization supports one standard protocol, no additional network configuration or third-party apps are required in order to connect Apple or Android devices to your VPN network. Also, a VPN can be configured manually or managed and configured per app, per profile, etc. A VPN is an important safeguard, particularly for private or highly sensitive information; it allows employees access to corporate resources anywhere in the world with an Internet connection and maintains security.

PART IV
COMPLIANCE

This section will help the internal auditors understand the compliance requirements related to smart devices. Chapter 16 will focus on compliance topics and will include regulations like the Health Insurance Portability and Accountability Act and the Payment Card Industry and will also discuss various compliance topics like litigation hold and e-Discovery. So, let's get started.

16

COMPLIANCE

16.1 Introduction

The use of smart devices within organizations adds a layer of complexity when it comes to regulatory compliance. For example, if an organization deals with health-related data, and that data are now housed within the smart device, the need to protect that information on the smart device is a requirement if they are to be compliant with regulations like the Health Insurance Portability and Accountability Act (HIPAA). Also, if you are a retailer and are accepting credit cards using smart devices, the requirement to secure the information on the smart device to be compliant with regulations like the Payment Card Industry (PCI) becomes necessary.

Although this chapter will discuss HIPAA and PCI requirements as they relate to the use of smart devices, there are other regulations that may apply to your organization. The basic principles of securing the information on the smart device remain similar.

16.2 HIPAA

In the good old days, the majority of us visited the hospitals and doctors and used to see those manila folders, which housed all the patients' history, being pulled from the large file cabinets by the front desk administrator. There was probably no backup kept of these folders, and, if one folder ever got lost, the historical information related to the patient was probably lost forever. Because of the paper form of the records, every time a health service provider (an x-ray technician or a healthcare specialist like a cardiologist or a podiatrist) had to view the patient's history, the primary doctor had to either fax the information or send the information via a regular postal service. This created an additional amount of paper copies. The risk of this paper form was obvious. The risk not only included the possibility of losing the file but also a potential compromise of paper records.

The security around the personal health of patients was minimal or nonexistent. In late 1990s, the federal government of the United States passed a law called the Health Insurance Portability and Accountability Act, which brought sweeping changes to the way the health provider and the health insurers did business. HIPAA was designed to protect the privacy and security of the patients' records, and the health industry had to go through a sweeping change in their security and privacy procedures.

In 2009, the federal government of the United States announced another healthcare law called Health Information Technology for Economic and Clinical Health Act (HITECH), which required health providers and insurers to convert the paper records to electronic records. The personal health information (PHI) residing on paper records became electronic personal health information (ePHI). While complying with this law, many health providers moved the ePHI to smart devices like tablets, and now you can see a large percentage of doctors running around with tablets when they see their patients.

With the proliferation of these devices within the healthcare industry, it raises the question of compliance. How are the health providers complying with the HIPAA and HITECH regulations? The federal government, through a website called healthIT.gov,* has provided several guidelines on how to protect and secure information when using a mobile device.

The HIPAA Security Rule requires covered entities to apply reasonable safeguards to protect PHI. The security rule requires appropriate administrative, physical and technical safeguards to ensure the confidentiality, integrity, and security of electronic protected health information. Some of the safeguards pertaining to mobile devices are listed as follows:

- *Administrative safeguards:* Administrative safeguards provide management, accountability, and oversight structure for covered entities to ensure that proper safeguards and policies and

---

* healthIT.gov is a website that has downloadable materials like posters, brochures, postcards, and other information related to compliance with the HIPAA and HITRUST.

procedures are in place to protect ePHI. Every organization must ask the following questions:

- Does the organization conduct periodic risk assessments on the use of smart devices?
- Does the organization have a documented and communicated smart device use policy?
- How does the organization make the users aware of their responsibilities? Does the organization have an awareness training program, and does the program contain a topic of smart device use?
- Does the organization allow personal devices to be used for ePHI exchange?
- How does the organization ensure that the ePHI is not altered or destroyed through authorized means?
- If the ePHI is stored in a cloud or with a third-party provider, is the risk assessment performed on the vendor?

- *Physical safeguards:* It is important to provide physical safeguards to protect the ePHI that is stored on and exchanged by smart devices. As smart devices are portable and smaller in size (compared to a laptop), they can be lost or stolen fairly easily. The Department of Health and Human Services' Office for Civil Rights repeatedly reports data breaches due to lost or stolen smart devices. Every organization must ask the following questions:
  - Does the organization have a process to inventory all smart devices, including the personal devices that are used to carry ePHI?
  - How do users protect their smart devices while travelling?
  - Does the organization use the latest technologies like radio-frequency identification tags on mobile devices, or does it use an outside service provider to locate lost or stolen devices?
  - Does the organization have the ability to remotely wipe, lock, or shut down the device?
  - What does the organization do when an employee or a user leaves the organization?

- *Technical safeguards:* Technical safeguards are the processes used to protect and control access to ePHI data. It is also used to protect the ePHI transmitted between a healthcare provider and a patient. Every organization must ask the following questions:

- Does the smart device provide encryption capabilities, or is there encryption on those smart devices that contain ePHI?
- Is there an appropriate antimalware software installed on the smart device?
- Does the smart device require the use of a firewall?
- Are the users provided the use of biometrics (and/or the password) to unlock the device? (This addresses the complaint from users that they want to keep the password simple so that they can enter the password while driving.)*
- Do the applications that transmit ePHI to a corporate network or third parties have secure channels (e.g., Secure Hypertext Transfer Protocol, virtual private network, secure tunnels)?

16.3 Payment Card Industry Data Security Standards

Everyone around us is starting to use smart device technology to accept credit cards. Whether it is your regular fashion store that swipes your card on a device connected to their iPad, or a furnace man who comes to your house and uses a *PayPal* device connected to his iPhone, or a cab driver who takes your credit card and swipes it to a *Square* device attached to his Android phone, the use of smart device technology in credit cards is becoming ubiquitous.

You may be thinking that, if they are doing it, why not your organization? Or your organization may take credit cards through your brick-and-mortar retail stores, and now you can get reports containing credit card information, which are visible on your smart device. What should an organization do?

The best place to start is the PCI Security Standards Council, which is an open global forum for the ongoing development, enhancement, storage, dissemination, and implementation of security standards for account data protection.†

---

* Of course, it is the opinion of the authors that the user should not be using the phone while driving—it is not only prudent but also probably against the law in most countries.
† http://www.pcisecuritystandards.org

The Payment Card Industry Security Standards Council's (PCI-SSC's) mission is to enhance payment account data security by driving the education and awareness of PCI Security Standards. The organization was founded by American Express, Discover Financial Services, JCB International, MasterCard, and Visa Inc.

Although the Payment Card Industry Data Security Standards (PCI-DSS) specifically do not have any requirements for smart devices, the controls required for protecting account data apply to the smart devices (in case the data reside on the smart card or if the smart card is used to accept credit cards). The PCI-DSS has also issued several guidelines on the topic of smart devices and credit card usage.

16.4 Off-the-Shelf Payment Acceptance Solution

The PCI-SSC highly recommends that the merchant who is going to accept the credit card payment use an off-the-shelf solution. The PCI-SSC provides a list of approved off-the-shelf vendors. These solutions already provide a point-to-point encryption (P2PE), which is the key to making sure that the credit card data are secure during the transaction. The diagram in Figure 16.1, acquired from the PCI-SSC website, shows how the approved PIN entry device (PED) and the approved card readers provide an end-to-end encryption.

The PCI-SSC website also mentions the following: "Validated P2PE solutions ensure that cardholder data is encrypted before it enters a mobile device. Using a validated and properly implemented P2PE solution greatly reduces the risk that a malicious person could

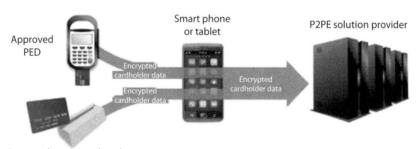

Figure 16.1   P2PE encrypt credit card data. (From https://www.pcisecuritystandards.org /documents/accepting_mobile_payments_with_a_smartphone_or_tablet.pdf?agreement=true &time=1471662830089, p. 1.)

intercept and use cardholder data. Solution providers will often provide you with a card reader that works with your mobile device. Validated solution providers will have a list of approved card readers (also called point of interaction or POI) that have been tested to work securely with their solution. The solution provider is responsible for ensuring that any POI used with their solution has been validated as compliant with the appropriate PCI-SSC security requirements, including the Secure Reading and Exchange of Data. Your solution provider will also tell you how to safeguard your mobile payment system. This guidance is contained in a P2PE Instruction Manual (PIM). Your acquirer or payment brand may ask you to complete a P2PE Self-Assessment Questionnaire as part of your annual PCI-DSS validation—including confirming that you are following the solution provider's PIM. You should coordinate with your acquirer or payment brand."*

16.5 Build Your Own Payment Acceptance Solution

If, for whatever reason (although those reasons are probably few and far between), you have decided to build your own payment acceptance solution, the PCI-DSS recommends that the POI device should be a PCI-DSS-approved device. According to the PCI-DSS website, "Mobile devices are not necessarily designed to be secure input or storage devices for cardholder data. Your mobile payment solution thus requires additional technology, including encryption, to secure cardholder data acceptance. The first part of a secure mobile payment solution is an approved 'point of interaction', which is the technical term for an approved PIN entry device (PED) or approved secure card reader (SCR) used to capture and encrypt cardholder data for a transaction. For example, the illustration above shows two options: one is a secure card reader (SCR) used to swipe the magnetic stripe of a payment card; the other is an approved PIN entry device (PED) for reading a card and manually entering a PIN. All these devices have a single purpose: to safely capture and encrypt cardholder data.

---

* https://www.pcisecuritystandards.org/documents/accepting_mobile_payments_with
  _a_smartphone_or_tablet.pdf?agreement=true&time=1471662830089, p. 1.

As additional devices become approved, they will be listed on the Council's website."*

Some of the action items we recommend, in addition to the PCI-DSS, are as follows:

- Ensure that the solution you pick is a P2PE solution.
- Where possible, use Europe Mastercard Visa technology. It is used more commonly in Europe and provides additional protection against fraud at the point-of-sale (PoS) registers by embedding a chip in the credit card. It provides an additional layer of authentication at the PoS to improve payment transaction security and reduce fraud.
- Check with your payment processor for recommendations. They may recommend solutions that you may not have considered.
- Ensure that no card data are stored on the mobile device.
- In terms of the device you deploy for payment card acceptance, ensure the following:
  - The device is not *rooted* or *jailbroken*.
  - Only those applications that have been approved by your organization or are from trusted sources are loaded on the device.
  - The smart device is updated with the latest version of the operating system. This will ensure that, if there are any known security vulnerabilities, they are patched.
  - The patch management process keeps the patches for the applications up to date.
  - The appropriate malware solution is installed on the device.
  - You are following the password policy of your organization for the smart device.

16.6 e-Discovery

Smart devices have become ubiquitous in both personal and business life. And it is one device that contains a lot of data that could potentially be detrimental to an organization during a litigation proceeding. Although smart devices will never be the key focus of an e-Discovery

---

* https://www.pcisecuritystandards.org/documents/accepting_mobile_payments_with _a_smartphone_or_tablet.pdf?agreement=true&time=1471662830089, p. 2.

request, they can definitely contain a piece of key evidence that can turn a potential victory into defeat.

The key evidence may be a text message by an executive, or a photo taken by a salesperson during an accident, or just the call history via call logs. All these data that reside on a smart device can provide that one piece of evidence that the opposing team may be looking for. Aside from the text messages, call logs, and photos, the following are some of the other potential data on a smart device that could be a part of e-Discovery:

- Contact list
- Videos
- Memos
- Voice mail
- Task list
- Calendar

The organizations should also consider that some smart devices allow the deleted data to be recovered using forensic tools, especially those smart devices that use subscriber identification module (SIM) cards.

Most of the time, an organization is legally allowed to search employees' devices, even if the device is owned by the employee. But, during those times when an employee does not agree to allow an organization to collect data from his or her smart device, it is not clear what an organization legally does. The privacy laws may not allow an organization to collect and search employees' personal data. It is important that, in such cases, the organization (or its general counsel's office) gets involved in the initial drafting of the smart device use policy.

16.7 Litigation Hold

The electronic stored information on the smart device is usually a backup to a media (disk or cloud). The litigation hold is usually put against the backup media when it comes to the smart device.

16.8 Export Regulations

The International Traffic in Arms Regulations (ITAR) and the Export Administration Regulations (EAR) are two important US export control laws that affect the manufacturing, sales, and distribution of technology.

The ITAR and EAR can restrict the use of smart devices (especially those devices that have built-in encryption). An organization should always check with the Websites* that are provided by these regulations to determine the latest and act accordingly.

16.9 Compliance Challenges

The privacy laws may limit the amount of control that an organization can have on the smart device, especially in those situations where the smart device is not owned by the organization.

---

* https://www.pmddtc.state.gov/regulations_laws/itar.html and https://www.bis.doc
.gov/index.php/regulations/export-administration-regulations-ear

PART V

REPORTING, MONITORING, AND AUDITING

This section will help the internal auditors understand the reporting, monitoring, and compliance requirements related to the smart devices. Chapter 17 will focus on these topics, and Chapter 18 will provide a sample of an audit plan.

So, let's get started.

17

REPORTING, MONITORING, AND AUDITING

17.1 Introduction

Once an organization starts to manage smart devices, it is important that appropriate reporting and monitoring are being conducted on their use and compliance with the organization's policy. This chapter will provide suggestions on some of the reporting and monitoring aspects.

17.2 Dashboard

Every organization should ensure that their smart device policies are being adhered to and that the smart devices are conforming to their use policy. One way to accomplish this is to use the dashboards provided by most mobile device management (MDM) solutions. These dashboards can be customized to showcase the key metrics required by an organization.

Some of the common metrics generally viewed by organizations are as follows:

- The number of devices that have not communicated to MDM software for certain days or weeks (as required by the organization's policy).
- The number of devices that have been reported lost or stolen.
- The number of devices locked due to incorrect passwords.
- The number of devices that are not meeting policy requirements:
  - Required level of operating system.
  - Blacklisted applications located on the device.
  - Antivirus software not installed.

Figure 17.1 Example of Microsoft Intune Dashboard.

- Wi-fi settings do not meet the policy requirements.
- Virtual private network settings do not meet the policy requirements.
- The number of devices identified as jailbroken or whose operating system has been compromised.

It is extremely important that an organization review these dashboards because, if some of these issues go unmonitored, they can introduce additional risks to the organization. It is also possible to set *alerts* based on the policy requirements so that the organization does not have to monitor the dashboard all the time, but can be notified via email or a text message if a certain situation arises (e.g., if a smart device is lost, the administrator is notified via an email and a text message).

Figure 17.1 shows an example of a dashboard from the Intune MDM software.

17.3 Auditing

The majority of MDM solutions provide auditing capabilities and assist you with the review of logs. Most MDM solutions can dump the log to other software like security information and event management (SIEM) and assist in auditing reports.

18
SAMPLE AUDIT PLAN

Prior to initiating the audit, the internal audit department should try to understand the smart device environment. At a minimum, the following information should be reviewed:

- How are the smart devices used within the organization?
- What security features are deployed on the devices?
- What information technology architecture is deployed to support the management of smart devices?
- What is the procedure of managing the smart devices?
- What reports are produced and reviewed to manage the smart devices?

Figure 18.1 lists the sample audit steps.

AUDIT/ASSURANCE PROGRAM STEP	CURRENT CONTROLS	GAPS	ACTION ITEMS
1. Planning and scoping the audit			
1.1 Define the audit/assurance objectives. The audit/assurance objectives are high level and describe the overall audit goals.			
1.2 Define the boundaries of review. The review must have a defined scope. The reviewer should understand the mobile devices in use by the enterprise, the data passing through these devices, and the relative risk to the organization.			
1.2.1 Obtain a list of mobile devices in use.			
1.2.2 Determine the scope of the review.			
1.3 Identify and document risks. The risk assessment is necessary to evaluate where audit resources should be focused. In most enterprises, audit resources are not available for all processes. The risk-based approach assures the utilization of audit resources in the most effective manner.			
1.3.1 Identify the business risk associated with mobile computing of concern to business owners and key stakeholders.			
1.3.2 Verify that the business risks are aligned with the IT risks under consideration.			
1.3.3 Evaluate the overall risk factor for performing the review.			
1.3.4 Based on the risk assessment, identify changes to the scope.			
1.3.5 Discuss the risks with management, and adjust the risk assessment.			
1.3.6 Based on the risk assessment, revise the scope.			
1.4 Define assignment success. The success factors need to be identified. Communication among the IT audit/ assurance team, other assurance teams, and the enterprise is essential.			
1.4.1 Identify the drivers for a successful review. (This should exist in the assurance function's standards and procedures.)			
1.4.2 Communicate success attributes to the process owner or stakeholder, and obtain an agreement.			

Figure 18.1   Sample audit steps.   *(Continued)*

AUDIT/ASSURANCE PROGRAM STEP	CURRENT CONTROLS	GAPS	ACTION ITEMS
1.5 Define the audit/assurance resources required. The resources required are defined in the introduction to this audit/assurance program.			
1.5.1 Determine the audit/assurance skills necessary for the review.			
1.5.2 Estimate the total audit/assurance resources (hours) and time frame (start and end dates) required for the review.			
1.6 Define the deliverables. The deliverable is not limited to the final report. Communication between the audit/assurance teams and the process owner is essential to assignment success.			
1.6.1 Determine the interim deliverables, including the initial findings, the status reports, the draft reports, the due dates for responses or meetings, and the final report.			
1.7 Communicate the process. The audit/assurance process must be clearly communicated to the customer/client.			
1.7.1 Conduct an opening conference to • Discuss the review objectives with the stakeholders • Obtain documents and information security resources required to effectively perform the review, and • Communicate timelines and deliverables			
2. Collect the following documents			
2.1 Smart Device Use Policy **2.2 Smart Device Security Policy** **2.3 IT infrastructure architecture documents** **2.4 MDM procedures** **2.5 Reports produced from MDM**			
3. Understand the smart device environment			
3.1 Is the device a corporate device or is bring your own device allowed? **3.2 Is the corporate data separated from the personal data?** **3.3 Is the personal use of the device allowed? (Can you play Angry Birds on your device?)** **3.4 Is an agreement in place where the employee abides with the corporate security policy?**			

Figure 18.1 (Continued) Sample audit steps.

(Continued)

AUDIT/ASSURANCE PROGRAM STEP	CURRENT CONTROLS	GAPS	ACTION ITEMS
3.5 Has the employee agreed to the remote wipe of the device management? 3.6 Can the record of their phone calls be viewed by corporate management? 3.7 Are confidential data residing on the device? If so, what are the procedures in place to monitor and control the confidential data? 3.8 What type of smart devices are allowed? Apple only? Android only? Others? 3.9 Is there a backup strategy and procedure in place for smart devices? 3.10 Is the smart device connecting to the corporate network? How is it being connected? 3.11 How are applications pushed to the device? Is the corporation developing its own apps? Do they have their own app store? Marketplace?			
4. Understand the IT architecture supporting the smart device environment			
4.1 Is the MDM solution a cloud-based solution or internally deployed? 4.2 Is the solution hosted by a third party or self-supported? 4.3 Is there a business associate agreement in place with the vendor?			
5. Understand the smart device security features			
5.1 Verify that the password policy is meeting industry standards. 5.2 Review the encryption requirements (especially for confidential data) and how encryption is deployed. 5.3 Is there a requirement for port controls on a device (camera usage, Bluetooth usage, Wi-fi controls)? 5.4 What procedure is in place for the remote wipe/locking and unlocking of a device? 5.5 What procedure is in place for the reporting of lost devices? 5.6 How are the devices tracked and monitored?			
5.7 What device configuration is pushed as a profile to the device (VPN, email, etc.)? 5.8 How is the delivery of applications controlled to the device? Does the corporation use blacklisting? Whitelisting? How are the features implemented? 5.9 What audit and monitoring features are turned on? What reports are being generated?			

Figure 18.1 (Continued)   Sample audit steps.   (*Continued*)

AUDIT/ASSURANCE PROGRAM STEP	CURRENT CONTROLS	GAPS	ACTION ITEMS
6. Understand how the smart devices are enrolled in the MDM software			
6.1 Does the organization use self-registry? How do users register their device? 6.2 How do users re-register when they purchase new device or replace an existing device? What happens to the old device? Are the data wiped off from the device? 6.3 How is it verified that the appropriate security policy has been pushed to the device?			
7. Understand how the smart devices are provisioned for email, contact, and address book			
7.1 How is email synced with the corporate servers? Is the email encrypted? 7.2 Where and how is virus checking performed?			
8. Understand how the applications are installed on the smart device			
8.1 Review the homegrown applications and how the data are stored and encrypted on the device. 8.2 Review the whitelisting and blacklisting deployment. 8.3 Review the authentication procedure for the applications—passwords? How are they authenticated? Is there an authorization process with corporate data?			
9. Understand how the smart devices are connected to the corporate network			
9.1 What type of remote connection is used? 9.2 What authentication is used prior to allowing access to corporate network? 9.3 What encryption protocols are in place for the remote connection?			
10. Understand the regulatory and compliance requirements related to smart device			
10.1 What reports and controls are in place to support the Health Insurance Portability and Accountability Act, the Sarbanes–Oxley Act of 2002, the Payment Card Industry, and other regulatory and compliance requirements?			

Figure 18.1 (Continued) Sample audit steps.   (*Continued*)

AUDIT/ASSURANCE PROGRAM STEP	CURRENT CONTROLS	GAPS	ACTION ITEMS
11. Understand the management reports that are produced related to smart devices			
11.1 What reports are reviewed by management? 11.2 What key statistics are monitored and reviewed?			
12. Understand the litigation and the litigation hold requirements			
13. Document the risks and produce the audit report			

Figure 18.1 (Continued) Sample audit steps.

PART VI
Sᴀᴍᴘʟᴇѕ

Sample: Smart Device Use and Security Policy

SMART DEVICE USE AND SECURITY POLICY

Administrative Provisions

Distribution:	All personnel
Issue Date:	Date
Effective Date:	Date
Issuer(s):	Name, Title, Division

Background

This policy describes the responsibilities of COMPANY's personnel while using the smart devices that are used to conduct COMPANY's business. Smart devices are devices like iPads, iPhones, and tablets running Android, Symbian, Windows, or other mobile operating systems. Smart devices are continuing to evolve and are becoming an important and integral part of mobility supported by COMPANY. With these smart devices come the risks of compromising COMPANY's critical assets, if these smart devices are lost, stolen, misplaced, or hacked. Failure to follow this policy exposes the COMPANY to a possible compromise of confidential data that could jeopardize COMPANY's public image, have a financial impact on COMPANY, or put the COMPANY in a possible violation of laws and regulations.

This policy is divided into two sections: one is the use policy, and the other is the security policy.

Use Policy

This policy outlines COMPANY's stance on how smart devices will be deployed and used within its enterprise. This policy covers different sections on which devices are allowed within COMPANY and how they are managed and used within COMPANY.

Supported Devices

In addition to BlackBerry, COMPANY will support devices that run iOS (e.g., iPhone and iPad) and Android devices. COMPANY IT will continue to monitor the marketplace of smart devices and update the supported devices as needed.

COMPANY-Owned Devices versus Employee-Owned Devices

COMPANY is investigating the pros and cons of allowing employees to bring their own devices and may allow these devices on an individual basis, but, at this time, only COMPANY-owned devices are supported.

Agreement

When the employee-owned device is connected to the COMPANY network, the employee will be required to sign off the USE POLICY FORM, which will allow COMPANY to perform functions on the device (e.g., select wipe or push VPN and PASSWORD policies on the device).

COMPANY Marketplace

COMPANY plans to deploy its own application marketplace where the approved applications for business use can be downloaded and installed. COMPANY may also push applications and updates to the smart devices as needed. COMPANY plans to deploy both custom applications and browser-based applications, which interface with existing applications.

Connection to COMPANY's Network

On an as-needed basis, COMPANY will allow selected smart devices to connect with COMPANY's network. COMPANY will ensure that all proper security profiles are pushed to the device for a secure connection. Employees must not try to alter and change these profile settings.

Personal versus Corporate Use Only
COMPANY expects its employees to conduct COMPANY business on the smart devices provided to its employees. Although it is understood that the smart device is the main form of communication for all employees, the COMPANY understands that the smart device will be used to conduct some personal business. However, each employee is required, as a part of the agreement (USE POLICY FORM), to comply with COMPANY's information security policies.

Confidentiality of Data
It is assumed that, during the normal use of smart devices, confidential data will be downloaded for viewing using these smart devices. The employees must adhere to the same security policies that they follow for desktop and/or laptop use.

Security Policy

This policy outlines COMPANY's stance on how smart devices will be secured. This policy covers the employee's responsibilities while using these smart devices. All employees are expected to exercise diligence and good judgment to secure the smart devices.

Security of Devices

- Password policy will be pushed to the smart device by COMPANY.
- Based on the information deployed on the smart device, COMPANY will determine the encryption requirements and push the implementation to the device.
- COMPANY may disable some ports of the device to comply with this policy (e.g., Bluetooth, camera, or Wi-fi).
- COMPANY will remotely wipe corporate data from the device, if the device is reported stolen. In some instances, where it may not be possible to wipe selected corporate data,

the entire content of the device may be wiped (depending on the security architecture deployed by COMPANY).

- COMPANY will be tracking the asset using GPS and other mechanisms.
- COMPANY plans to push device configuration policies for VPN, Wi-fi, and email to the device. It is expected that employees will not attempt to change these settings.
- COMPANY will determine the mechanisms of pushing mobile applications and updates to the device. Employees are expected to have the device connected to COMPANY network so that such deployment is possible.
- COMPANY, at its discretion, may use the whitelisting or blacklisting of applications. Whitelisting allows only *selected* applications to run on the device, whereas blacklisting does not allow identified applications to be run on the device.
- COMPANY will deploy tools and processes to comply with the regulatory and audit requirements for the smart devices. Employees must not attempt to change the settings of these parameters.

Sample: Smart Device Use Policy Form

Purpose

The purpose of this form is to define the agreement between the COMPANY and the employees who want to use their own mobile device to connect to COMPANY's network. This form is to be signed in conjunction with COMPANY's *Smart Device Acceptable Use Policy* and the *Smart Device Security Policy*.

As indicated in the use policy and the security policy, the overriding goal is to protect the confidentiality and integrity of COMPANY's data. Therefore, all users who are connecting their own personal device to COMPANY's network must agree to the following:

- Password policy will be pushed to the smart device by COMPANY. Employees will have to comply with the password rules and other parameters outlined in the password policy.
- Based on the information deployed on the smart device, COMPANY will determine the encryption requirements and push the implementation to the device. Employees will not be able to override the encryption implementation.
- COMPANY may disable some ports of the device to comply with this policy (e.g., Bluetooth, camera, or Wi-fi). Employees will not be able to enable these ports once the COMPANY disables the ports.
- COMPANY will remotely wipe corporate data from the device, if the device is reported stolen. In some instances, where it may not be possible to wipe selected corporate data, the entire content of the device may be wiped. (Depending on the security architecture deployed by COMPANY, this statement should be updated.) This includes all the personal data of the employee on the device. *It is recommended that employees back up their personal data frequently to minimize loss if a remote wipe is necessary.* A remote wipe will only be initiated if the IT deems it absolutely necessary. The examples of situations requiring remote wipe include, but are not limited to, the following:
  - Theft of the device
  - Loss of the device

- Termination of employment in which the employee has not already cleared corporate data by another method
- COMPANY will be tracking the asset using GPS and other mechanisms.
- COMPANY plans to push device configuration policies for VPN, Wi-fi, and email to the device. It is expected that employees will not attempt to change these settings.
- COMPANY will determine the mechanisms of pushing mobile applications and updates to the device. Employees are expected to have the device connected to COMPANY network so that such deployment is possible.
- COMPANY, at its discretion, may use the whitelisting or blacklisting of applications. Whitelisting allows only the *select* applications to run on the device, whereas blacklisting does not allow identified applications to be run on the device. This may force employees to run only *allowed* applications on your device.
- COMPANY will deploy tools and processes to comply with the regulatory and audit requirements for the smart devices. Employees must not attempt to change the settings of these parameters.

Applicability

Employees who do not wish to connect their smart devices to COMPANY's resources are free to refuse to sign this waiver. The waiver only applies to the employees and devices that have accessed company resources.

Employee Declaration

I, EMPLOYEE, have read and understood the above Smart Device Use Policy Form, and consent to have my device wiped if COMPANY's IT department deems it necessary.

_____   _____
Employee Signature   Date

_____   _____
Manager Signature   Date

Sample: Minimum Smart Device Configuration Security Standard

MINIMUM SMART DEVICE CONFIGURATION SECURITY STANDARD

Administrative Provisions

Distribution:	All personnel
Issue Date:	July 21, 2016
Effective Date:	July 21, 2016
Issuer(s):	Name, Title, Division

Background

This standard describes the minimum smart device security configuration of COMPANY's personal smart devices while accessing corporate resources. Smart devices are devices like iPads, iPhones, and tablets running Android, Symbian, Windows, or other mobile operating systems. Smart devices are continuing to evolve and are becoming an important and integral part of mobility supported by COMPANY. With these smart devices come the risks of compromising COMPANY's critical assets, if these smart devices are lost, stolen, misplaced, or hacked. Failure to follow this configuration standard exposes the COMPANY to a possible compromise of confidential data that could jeopardize COMPANY's public image, have a financial impact on COMPANY, or put the COMPANY in possible violation of laws and regulations.

Passcodes

1. Passcodes should be required on all smart devices that will access corporate resources.
2. Smart devices should require complex passcodes. (Passcodes should require at least one letter, one number, a special character, and at least one uppercase and one lowercase letter.)
3. Passcodes should be at least six characters long.
4. Passcodes should expire every 90 days and require your users to create a new passcode.

5. Users should be required to create a different passcode after expiration, to prevent your users from using the same two or three passcodes over and over.

6. Devices should automatically erase all data from the device in the event that 10 or less incorrect passcodes are entered.

7. The device should automatically lock after 5 minutes or less with no user interaction.

Encryption

8. All smart devices that access corporate resources should require that the device is encrypted. (For all Apple iOS devices with a passcode, encryption is enabled by default. Android devices should require that encryption is enabled. Android and other platform smart devices that do not support encryption should not be allowed to access corporate resources.)

Restrictions

9. Smart devices should disallow accessing Siri or other similar services when the device is locked.

10. Devices should be nondiscoverable via Bluetooth.

11. Documents/photos/videos should not automatically sync to unapproved cloud services.

Index

Page numbers followed by f and t indicate figures and tables, respectively.